I0554633

THE MENTALITY OF THE PROPHET'S STAFF

Ken Cox

REJOICE
Essential Publishing

Ken Cox/Rejoice Essential Publishing
PO BOX 512
Effingham, SC 29541
www.republishing.org

Unless otherwise indicated, scripture is taken from the King James Version.

The Mentality of the Prophet's Staff/Ken Cox

ISBN-13: 978-1-956775-73-0

TABLE OF CONTENTS

DEDICATION

This book is dedicated to anyone who dares to be different. Being different is not always a curse, nor is it always a burden either. I have found that being different is what it is. Being different is the reality of relationship legacy. Those of you who have been chosen to carry a prophetic staff should give God the praise because you have been chosen to be different.

In 2017, when I wrote *"The Prophetic Staff,"* I was excited and ready to change the prophetic community with what God had given me. Many who read the book looked at me and said ok. For some, it was their way of falling out with me; for others, it spurred the argument they wanted to have with me to stop.

What I wrote was different, and some did not understand or could accept what God was doing. Yes, it was different, but it was scriptural and in the will of God. Remember that we must be different to be who He has called us to be. Not all prophets/seers have this calling. Let me be clear.

It is now in mid-2023, now six years later. Yes my God, has been good to me. This is the long-awaited follow-up to *"The Prophetic Staff."* Thank you so much to those who have walked this walk with me. My wife, Prophetess Sabina Cox and the Where Eagles Fly family, and a handful of close friends, who know who they are. Prophets, I thank you for your patience as you waited for me to understand what I will share.

I decided to stand, and if I lost along the way, I knew God would bless the remnant of my life that was left. He has proven that to me. I am thankful because they who were hard on me because of the Prophet's Staff helped me to become who I am today. They showed me another level of the precious process of growing and I simply never want to stop that growth.

This book is about the mentality of carrying a staff. This book is about you and I. This is how personal you want to be with God. I dedicate this to those who are confident to carry a prophetic staff.

You know that God has called you to this unique type of ministry. Those of you who may not have this special call upon your life will also benefit from this book as we discuss the mental aspect of The Ministry of the Prophetic Staff. Prophet, know that because of your staff, yes you will deal with the stares and misunderstandings that have been directed at Apostles and Prophets forever.

This includes our prophetic peers sometimes. You will learn to overlook much for the cause and purpose of God upon your life. Trust me when I say that! This is one of those issues that you have to be bigger than because of the God within you.

Prophet, it is my honor to dedicate this book to you. I pray that this book clarifies your assignment and what and why God has called you to carry a prophetic Staff. Please open your mind and understand the effect of your mentality as you employ a Prophetic Staff in your ministry. This book will open you to becoming the best version of yourself. It will take that to employ *The Mentality of the Prophet's Staff.*

CHAPTER 1

SEAT 23D AND MY STAFF

The title of this chapter says it all for me; allow me to explain. I am on a plane for my next engagement, and I have to settle for seat 23D. Seat 23D is an aisle seat, but I am still cramped and complaining to myself. Why did I book this? Why did I settle for this when I know who I work for and how He cares and has blessed me?

Seat 23D taught me a lesson that I will never forget. Whenever the opportunity to book 1st class or secure a private flight comes, seize it. This will make a difference in my life and my assigned work. Well, how does that fit with my Prophetic Staff, you ask? Six years ago, I wrote on the Prophetic Staff, and there was so much I did not know to include. Like seat 23D on the plane, I knew there was more to share, and I had to be the first partaker.

What am I saying? This is personal, and I needed a deposited experience of what I am sharing to allow you to grow as you read this. I realize this is far bigger than I am, so allow me to vent as you swallow this information.

Let's start at *1 Timothy 4:1-3*. The Spirit of God expressly says in our now latter times, some will depart from the faith. Clearly, this is us prophets as we are giving heed to spirits of deception, the very doctrines of demons. These spirits speak lies. I want to think that we all know that.

Prophets, it is no secret that the Spirit makes it clear that some will give up on the faith as time passes. Invariably there will be liars in life. They lie so much until their lies seem so true.

We have prophets and people like that in this era we live in. They will tell you things like you should not get married. They'll tell you not to eat this or that food, and of course, they will tell you not to listen to the prophet, including some prophets who listen to no one! These prophets are self-appointed experts on everything except themselves.

Today over and over, it seems to take a falling to take heed of what God has spoken. We, as prophets, see our lives are now being lived out in weakness, frustration, and bad attitudes because someone has prophesized us out of the will of the Lord. And to put the icing on the cake, we are too proud to admit it. I often think of prophets who have demonstrated the ability to be unstable, weak, and wishy-washy.

Make no mistake about it. There are thousands of unknown prophets who carry the call of God but have not been encouraged to do anything about it. Instead, they sit in churches worldwide, trying to be faithful to a system that will not encourage and release them into their destinies. Yes, if you are carrying a Prophetic Staff, you need to know and embrace this.

Prophet, in general, you need to know that it will cost you everything to answer the call of God fully! And to know it is all worth it seems to be a lost prospect. Prophets who are totally fulfilled in the calling of God know what they are doing and what they have been called to do. This is what the ministry of the staff brings to your life.

You may very well be an outsider among your peers, and you need to learn and accept this. Let this be one of your first lessons.

Prophets, stop expecting every other prophet or Christian to recognize God's calling on you. They won't. What most of us as prophets today fail to understand the more you are in the center of God's will, the more you will be questioned and misunderstood.

That is why it is so important that we, as prophets, hear from God for ourselves and live with the conviction of His voice in our hearts day by day. This is why you need to know you have heard from God on your assignment to carry a prophetic staff.

A big part of our annual problem is that we connect to many toxic relationship behaviors that are baked right into our culture but not God's plan for our lives. Read this carefully, prophet, and take inventory. Every year we worship the idea of being accepted and esteemed, and we entangle carefree in what we call divine relationships before we even truly know each other. This does not work and never will.

1 Thessalonians 5:12-13 says, "I beseech you prophet, that you will know them which labor among you, and are over you in the Lord." Prophet, you are admonished prophet; you must learn how to esteem leaders in love for their work's sake. Living and being at peace among yourselves is a valuable key to carrying the prophetic staff. This is called respect for your assignment.

Unfortunately, because we have so many prophets who want to and seem to desire to build their mental strength against all things that are toxic, they often miss God's plan for their life. The theme of this chapter is personal with me and personal with and for you. We must be in the right place and frame of mind to carry a prophetic staff and be effective.

This assignment is for mentally strong prophets who know they are called by God. Please understand that not every mentally strong prophet will carry a staff. Again I stress if you are chosen, then embrace it. I wasted time as I felt sorry for myself as I sat on seat 23D. I knew I should have been in a different part of the plane, but I settled and then had to nerve to complain to God and myself repeatedly.

I lost the opportunity for a better seat and settled. My discomfort caused me to understand this was my personal issue, which I needed to overcome. Carrying a prophetic staff is personal, and if you are fortunate to be a part of a group like *Where Eagles Fly LLC*. The bonus is we have multiple prophets who carry staffs, and we also realize not all do or will.

Understand that, more often than not, you may not have a group of prophets around you to back you up as you carry a staff. Prophet, again this is so personal, and you must embrace your assignment as you go forth. Let's talk about the Seat 23D's in your life. Who are they, and what do they represent? We will call them the ten basic common types of toxic relationships you, as a mentally strong prophet, should avoid.

Please notice I said a mentally strong prophet; this is the qualifier as you move into your prophetic career. We must know to avoid the following ten types of relationships that I will discuss. Your life is far too important to God because of what you carry. This is why you will need to know about these different types of relationships that will weigh on your ability to be different. Let's discuss them now.

1. Relationships will be run by one person.

A relationship is toxic when one person is running it. Period. There should be no debate here, none. Sometimes a prophet will feel out of control or lost. This can be unhealthy looking to someone willing to take charge of your life. This is for you to alleviate the pressure. Now consider that God has called you to carry a prophetic staff; this will hinder your walk. Before you do consider this, keep reading.

Imagine putting a collar around your neck and handing the leash to someone else; you'll have no say about where they lead you. And then you want to complain to other prophets and whoever else will listen. The relationship between Jezebel and her prophets is a classic example of this. Are you affected by this type of relationship?

This is not mentorship for a prophet; it is the Jezebel Anointing at its finest. Prophets should never feel powerless or trapped in a relationship because they will not grow. In fact, if either prophet feels powerless or trapped, a relationship doesn't exist.

Healthy prophetic relationships are built on a solid foundation of mutual respect, trust, free will, and teamwork, even if you are different.

Prophetic relationships are one of the greatest vehicles of personal prophetic growth. Prophets achieve far more by working with others. The strength of each prophet determines the quality of any prophetic relationship. Again, one prophet may carry a staff, while the other prophet may not. Prophets, it is not always a given that your peers will carry a staff.

2. When relationships are supposed to "complete" you.

Our culture is predicated on many fantasies. Many prophets seem to always want to blame another prophet or person for why you aren't moving forth. It's not your 's job, your mentor's job, or anyone else's job to fill in your empty voids. This is the essence of being different and not fitting the status quo.

That's your job, prophet, and yours alone. You will never grow until you accept full responsibility for your emptiness, pain, or boredom; these types of problems will inevitably ensue in every one of your relationships, including your relationship with God. Can you see yourself carrying a prophetic staff with this burden upon you?

God is your source, and His love completes you. Moses found this out during his 40 years in the wilderness; Elijah, Elisha, Anna, and Deborah are all examples of a relationship with God that completes their life and sends people into their life to help complete and mature their ministry.

3. Relationships that rely on prophetic peer codependency.

Do your actions and thoughts revolve around another prophet? Do you or that prophet dismiss completely disregard your own needs? That's codependency, and it's toxic. Do your personal needs go out the window because some get mad? Prophet, it's not your responsibility to make one another feel better. This type of mentality will kill your focus on who you are and what you are called to do, especially when walking with a prophetic staff.

This is not prophetic growth when suddenly, neither one of you can plan something without getting approval from the other because you're so tight. Can you see yourself needing your buddy's approval for something God has given you? Think long and hard about this. We see it so much, and when the prophets fall out, and they will, it then wants everyone's attention to prove who is right versus who is wrong.

The biggest problem prophets have as they develop codependent tendencies that breed resentment. Let's look at this. Prophetess A is mad and upset. Prophetess B is the recipient of the anger of Prophetess A. All this is because she's had a challenging day, is aggravated, and needs attention; that's understandable. Let us consider if it becomes an expectation that your life revolves around her emotional well-being 24/7. Eventually, Prophetess B is going to become bitter towards Prophetess A and her feelings and desires.

"The greatest gifts you can give another prophet is love and your own personal development. This is the basis of empowerment, taking care of yourself so you can serve others for God as they do the same for you. When you make the choice to reveal to the world that you will carry a prophetic staff, this will be the healthy relationship you will seek in your life.

Prophet, you must take responsibility for your own emotions and expect your brother and sister prophet to be responsible for theirs. That is different from being supportive to being always obligated. Jeremiah is an example; he had to deal with himself, and his seclusion was a tool God used to deal with him, and it matured and grew him into a prophet worthy of God sending to the Nations.

4. Relationships based on idealistic expectations.

Prophet, we don't love and appreciate someone because they're perfect; you love and appreciate them despite them not being perfect.

"Perfection" is a deadly fantasy none of us will ever obtain, but our perfection as prophets is maturity.

Allow yourself and other prophets to be perfectly imperfect. Stop trying to fix every prophet you meet because they do not fit in your prophetic model of how you see and view other prophets. They are perfectly imperfect, just the way they should be. Your carrying a staff will be perfectly imperfect.

No one prophet in your life will act exactly as you hope or expect them to, ever. They are not you, and they will not love, give, understand, or respond as you do. Remember, you are different. For a prophet, misplaced expectations are killers. Elijah, with his misplaced expectations at his miracles of slaying hundreds of prophets of Baal and calling fire down from heaven. He expects everyone will be saved, but everyone is not.

Prophets, our ability to temper unrealistic expectations, is critical. How they or it "should be" will significantly reduce frustration and suffering. Prophet's real relationships will never be perfect, but if you're willing to work at it and open up, it could be everything you've ever dreamed of. Think about this as you now carry a prophetic staff and consider the unreal expectations that may be passed around your circle of influence.

5. Relationships that feature past blame to justify present righteousness.

Prophetic peers and people who continue to blame you for your past mistakes are saying to you the relationship is toxic. How many of us have been called to different realms of the prophetic, and you are a victim of past issues or mistakes?

Prophets, as you do this to each other to try and justify their own present righteousness, you are both in a lose-lose situation. You're dodging your current issues, and you're digging up guilt and bitterness from the past. Your goal is to manipulate the other person into feeling wrong in the present.

If this goes on long enough, both prophets in the relationship suffer. Both prophets will spend most of their energy trying to prove one is less guilty than the other rather than solving the issue. You must recognize that in our relationships with each other, we are connected to all of their prior mistakes, and vice versa. Prophet, if you don't accept those mistakes, then ultimately, you do not accept them. Once again, this relationship will have you in a bitter place, and you will be locked in self-pity. You will not be effective with a staff. Your focus will be off.

Moses had to lead a nation of people who revered him, talked about him, and ridiculed him but wanted to blame him at the drop of a hat for everything. Imagine how they talked about him and why they followed him, and why he was thought to be inadequate.

Does anyone remember what happened after the 12 went up and brought back a bad report? You now have been chosen by God to carry a prophetic staff in the now day generation. You can fall prey to blaming others for what has happened or be the one who self-elevates yourself because you want to prove something. Either way, you will miss the mentality needed to be effective and a now-generation prophet who has been called to carry a prophetic staff.

6. Relationships that are built on day-to-day lies.

Trust is the prophetic foundation of a healthy relationship, especially in the prophetic. Trust, when broken, requires time and willingness on the part of both people to repair it and heal. All too often, we start hearing multiple stories about a person who we have fallen out with. Other relationships are built, and story and story are told to strengthen new relationships and to justify past actions. Do not fall for this prophet.

Welcome to the unstable and unpredictable world of prophetic contradictions, as omissions and outright lies. Many prophets today have found out that covering up your tracks along the way does not work. Somewhere the truth is revealed, and trust in the relationship is broken, and then smear campaigns are started to build and maintain existing relationships.

Prophets an honest adversary is always better than a prophetic friend who lies to you. Remember that. Prophet you by virtually carrying a prophetic staff will have honest adversaries. This is a fact, so get over it.

Right here, understand that you will have to pay less attention to what people say and more attention to what they do. Their actions will show you the truth in the long run. Prophets, stop allowing prophetic peers to lie to you. Your ability to carry a prophetic staff is built on how you handle relationships in your life.

Don't partake in their nonsense and ridicule of others. Don't let their lies be your reality, especially when you don't have all the facts. Don't be afraid to stand up for the truth. You want forgiveness and reconciliation; it can't begin until this truth is told. Can you see how your thinking may be clouded?

Think of the prophets who knew Amos and could not stand him because he told the truth. Think of the ones who talked about his heritage, his previous occupation and did not want him around because he was a prophet of character.

7. Relationships lacking forgiveness and the willingness to rebuild trust.

Prophets when trust is broken, which happens in life, it's essential to understand that it can be repaired, provided all concerned are willing to do the hard work of self-growth. Many prophetic relationships have hit the solid bedrock bottom and crumbled into dust.

This was because prophets can be so stubborn and unwilling. Prophets need to take advantage of the opportunities to shed the patterns and dynamics with each other that led to the relationship's failure.

Prophets, this is painful work. Broken trust is always hard to repair. Life teaches us that trust levels rise and fall over time if we can figure out how to hold on and grow together. This is why your walk as a prophet who carries a staff is so personal and the inner work you must be willing to do.

Do you understand it took Moses 40 years to do the inner work within himself? Prophetess Deborah lived and worked in a time when women were looked upon as second-class citizens, and she had to deal with her hurt and yet trust men and still be willing to do what God called her to do. Mentally can you see her point? Unless you understand your calling is more significant than you, it is reasonable to find you in a place of emotional stress.

8. Relationships in which passive aggression trumps communication.

Prophetic Passive-aggressive behavior will assume many forms. Those forms can generally be non-verbal aggression that manifests in negative behavior. It happens with leaders, peers, and subordinates. Instead of openly expressing how they feel, prophets make subtle, annoying gestures directed at prophetic peers or leadership. Instead of saying what's upsetting you, we often do it another way. We will embrace small and petty ways to take jabs at someone. Then they pay attention and get upset. Most of you will be exposed to this as you carry your prophetic staff.

This behavior clearly shows that two people or prophets are not comfortable communicating openly and clearly with one another. A prophet does not have to be passive-aggressive. That prophet, if they feel safe expressing any worries or insecurities within the relationship. A prophet should never have to hide behind passive aggression. Especially when and if that prophet feels like they won't be judged or criticized for what they are thinking, and that is fair.

Healthy prophetic relationships, feelings, and desires are shared openly; this is called family. Prophets must learn how to make it clear. The other person or prophet may not be necessarily obligated to your ideas and opinions. This is fair, and you would love to have their support. There will be some type of compromise in some way.

The prophetess Huldah no doubt faced this as a female prophet in a male-dominated era she lived in. She was different, and know that you will be different, also in many circles, as you walk with a prophetic staff. Every prophetic peer may not seek to have a healthy relationship with you, and you must understand this. We all are not on the same level in this manner. We have discussed this point, and again it comes back to you and how you choose to handle yourself.

9. Prophetic relationships by emotional blackmail.

Emotional blackmail is dangerous. Emotional blackmail is when someone applies an emotional penalty. That is an emotional penalty against you when you don't do exactly what they want. The key condition here is that behavior changes, against your will, because of the emotional blackmail. Emotional blackmail makes a prophet do things a certain way as you fear the penalty, so you give in. The prophet who carries a staff must know and embrace this about themself and others.

Prophets should always be able to have an honest conversation when their prophetic peers do not understand what God has them doing. This is crucial for prophets in a relationship. We need to know that our quiet negative thoughts and feelings can be talked out safely to one another. There do not have to be penalties or harsh repercussions. Otherwise, prophets will suppress their true thoughts and feelings. Yes, this will stifle your growth, which leads to an environment of distrust and manipulation. We see this so much in today's prophetic arena.

Prophets, we all get upset at someone we care about or we do not like something about them. That's called being an imperfect human being.

Understand that committing to a prophetic or apostolic leader and always liking that leader's choices is not the same thing, by no means. One can be committed to someone and not like everything about them, and it works vice versa.

On the contrary, senior and mature prophets who can communicate sincere criticism towards one another are special. They do it without judgment, or emotional blackmail will strengthen their commitment. This requires mature prophets to communicate with one another in the long run. Aaron was a better prophet to Moses because of what he dealt with in that position. The conflict of being an older brother and prophet to God's prophet to the nations was a sign that sincere communication was needed.

Let's note right here that the prophetic staff was a part of who Moses was, and he carried his staff everywhere. Today you may not carry your staff everywhere, but the same respect needs to be given even when we do not understand or disagree.

10. Relationships that are always put on the back burner.

When prophets and prophetic leaders fail to carve out quality time for important relationships, we know this is one of the most toxic relationship mistakes we can make in our lives. This goes unnoticed most of the time until everything starts falling apart.

Relationships require dedicated time to survive and thrive. This is cut and dry. It's easy to allow life to take over, especially when you have ministry obligations, family, and a need to rest.

Prophets, you must make time every week to do this. Your focus has to be felt by those who you care about. Every day find time to pour out. Do this even when you have just a few moments of quality interaction into your closest relationships.

The building of this type of relationship is critical. We see this as the prophets who carry staffs and are effective display a mentality that aligns with having value within their relationships. Remember this will benefit you greatly.

Prophets, nothing you can give is more appreciated than your sincere, focused attention. Your presence is everything. When we value our relationships, prophetic peers know it and will respond.

Do you see what seat 23D did for me? It opened me up to an understanding of who was around me and how I had to ID them. For me, it was not the people; it was my mentality toward them and myself. How I responded, and how what was my normalcy changed. Let me be clear. It has been six years since I wrote on the prophetic staff. I have grown, and you will also. Seat 23D was the positioning for release. Your positioning may come in any way God sees fit.

Now as we discuss Chapter 2, let's get even more personal as we start to make the necessary changes mentally as we prepare to carry the prophetic staff, or maybe you have a staff, and you are wondering what your next move is. The first thing we must do is accept moving away from our self-appointed normalcy.

MOVING AWAY FROM MY SELF-NORMALCY

Your gifts are given by the Spirit to empower you to bless others. Sometimes you will encourage and give life-giving words to others. Sometimes you may activate the gift of teaching. Sometimes deliverance, but the reality is that our prophetic gifts are diverse, given for the benefit of others. This is what is troublesome when we fail to understand that our gifts facilitate change.

The reality is if you're a prophet, God has given you gifts. Your gift may be different than mine, but as you just read in Chapter 1, respect and value will open divine doors of understanding. This includes your walking with a prophetic staff. Some people will, and some people won't.

That is not your problem; your issue is understanding how to move forward with your assignment. This will move you through a process that will take you from your comfort of normalcy.

When God uses a prophet that has been through a maturing process, you see the prophet knows how to steward their gifts effectively. A prophet should know their talents, time, energy, and enthusiasm are for the good of others and the glory of God. This is not for the prophet who has a staff and has allowed their staff to be a house or ministry decoration.

You, prophet, if you're going to do this, you will see your normal changed. There are some identifying factors that stop a prophet's life from being normal. Because a prophet is gifted, they may experience early success and little or no failure, while others may struggle.

The prophet may see the rapid advancement of their gift, and people may be blessed and empowered. The application of giftedness ultimately determines who becomes genuinely successful. This is what will separate a prophet from those who are simply playing the role of a prophet and those who struggle to employ the skills to maximize their gifts.

These prophets often find that their inborn or natural talent is no longer sufficient to be successful. Things that were easy to them now are not. Many prophets never learn the skills of Godly success. These skills are birthed by hard work, persistence, patience, perseverance, and discipline. Success is not up for debate because many people, including prophets, describe it differently.

Success is a mentality; it is a mindset. This is what the mentality of the prophetic staff is all about. I am not here to flatter you with Jewish and Hebrew folklore but to help elevate your mindset to be effective because you are different. This is my assignment with this book.

This includes those of you who use a prophetic staff and those of you who do not. I expressed this in the dedication of this book, and it is still a factor. Do not overlook it.

The issue here is that being successful will expose the prophet's life to a loss of normalcy. As a prophet, your life now becomes a targeted criticism by peers, family, and of course, by people you may have never known. Let's assume you have been called to carry a prophetic staff, and all these factors in your life multiply.

Consider your arena of routine and your decision; your obedience has cost you greatly. Your ability to work the work of the prophetic ministry will make you a target of people and peers who will want to use you. Some for the employment of your gifts, some for your covenant connections, and others for your unique ability to operate in the fullness of what God has simply called you to do.

There will be many who will expose themselves in a magnitude of ways. Peers and people will want your loss of normalcy to be for their gain and not yours. The reality of everybody having an opinion of you becomes real. You will think you do not matter, but behind your back, you will be a vital part of constant conversation and criticism.

They will use your being known as the key to making assumptions about you. Your carrying the prophetic staff will multiply that. Your very loss of normalcy is the rope they use to make the attachment of issues and talk of why you now carry a staff. This is true in significant personal and ministry relationships for prophets, like with their parents, siblings, friends, bosses, and especially other intimate relationships with peers. Are you ready to handle this or not is my question?

Why do opportunities arise when a prophet moves from an unknown prophetic ministry to becoming known? Are not all these opportunities from God? Look at it. If you buy into our culture's view of giftedness, then it can be as much of a burden as a blessing. At the same time, giftedness is a wonderful opportunity to accomplish great things.

One of the great burdens we create in the Body of Christ is who we identify as being gifted for what. All are gifted, but not all are gifted alike. How many times have you seen or told someone they were gifted for something they really are not? We now put unnecessary pressure on someone, and there is no point in labeling. People will always do this. You need to know this and keep your mind set on your assignment. Therefore, the prophet who operates and carries a prophetic staff today must have themself together mentally.

The key point is whether gifted or not; there's nothing they can do about it anyway. Leaders must be honest and let gifted people, such as prophets, know that they're blessed to have the gift but love them enough to tell them it is only a starting point. Whether it is ever fully realized is entirely up to them. This helps prophets in the battle for normalcy in their lives. Your carrying a prophetic staff in your ministry will keep you humble and hungry for God. This is a starting point, as many of you read this in your walk with your prophetic staff.

The single most significant predictor of a prophet's success remains how devoted to the relationship with God they are and the activity of the gift. In *1 Samuel Ch. 3*, the more Samuel practiced, the better he became. Hard work means putting in the necessary time, sticking with it when it's not always fun, persevering in the face of setbacks and failures, and developing all the skills necessary to succeed. This is the ministry of the prophet. This is also the blueprint for how you will learn the ministry of the staff.

A gifted prophet will have an advanced capacity to learn, whether they employ it or not. A gifted prophet of God will depend on the opportunities that are offered. In fact, it is not unusual for a gifted prophet to achieve poor grades in ministry work and purposely do dumb things if they think their capacities will show them in a bad light to their peers. This is why some gifted prophets struggle with peer pressure and overall disabilities. This is what will and has happened to many prophets.

The hard reality is that there must be a radical pursuit of God. Mature prophets are submitted prophets. These type of prophets have realized that losing the sense of normalcy that others enjoy is not a disqualification. This is acceptance for them. They understand that God demands consecration to His purpose and willingness to do and accomplish any assignment. This is the essence of the call unto death that prophets live with. *Philippians 1:20* says that a dead man is a dangerous man; we are dangerous to many. When we are dead to the world and alive in Christ, we can't be intimidated or threatened.

It is no secret that prophets are recognized by their dress, habits, and lifestyles. This will include your walking with a prophetic staff. The consistent holiness of your character is what will identify you prophet before God; this is the essence of the relationship God is looking for in His prophets. This is true, whatever your assignment is.

Jeremiah is a classic example of losing a sense of normalcy in a prophet's life. The repercussions in His life were difficult. Those of you who are struggling with your choice of walking with a staff, read and reread Jeremiah. He was alienated from family and friends and was rejected by his community. He also saw the loss of his people, who lost land and a temple they firmly believed was promised to them by God.

Welcome to Jeremiah's world. You must decide if you're going to see this through. Jeremiah preaches for over 40 years, and we see this in his life as he details deep personal anguish at the trials and tribulations of his calling. *"Woe is me,"* he says, *"a man of strife and con-*

tention to the whole land," adding a wish that he had not even been born *(Jeremiah 15:10)*.

Jeremiah is tortured by his role as a prophet, identifying with God and Judah, whom he believes God is punishing. Prophet, who do you identify with? You're now carrying a staff, or maybe you will start soon and you are under attack. You feel a sense of loss.

Loss, for prophets, is necessary, and Jeremiah was the classic example; like the defeat of Judah, and the destruction of the temple, Jeremiah was confident that God would restore not merely the nation but the very heart of its people, reconciling them to God, to land, and to each other.

The loss meant purpose in Jeremiah's eyes: restoration, Jeremiah 30–31. On a personal level, Jeremiah experiences a loss of his integrity as a prophet among his own people. God has called him to say things that he wished he didn't have to say, things that made him unpopular as a prophet.

As far as the nation was concerned, Jeremiah viewed the loss as a necessary punishment and a painful means to correct the human-divine relationship. This is not normal. This is not what prophets today want to do. The prophet's personal sacrifices, like Jeremiah, ruin the sense of normalcy in one's life.

In *Jeremiah 16:2*, the call of the prophetic required Jeremiah to remain single. God says to Jeremiah, *"You will never marry. You will have no children."* In *Jeremiah 16:5-9*, he was to refrain from attending social events, such as funerals and weddings. Jeremiah's whole life is consumed with fulfilling his prophetic role. Prophet, are you willing to consume your life for the purposes of God if that means you carry a prophetic staff? Does it mean that much to you? Can you relate?

Who wants the Jeremiah anointing? Do you? Let's look at the absence of a spouse or family and no social events. This, on the outside looking in, is a thankless and despised profession. The fact that he could continue to live his life, let alone remain obedient to the Lord speaks volumes.

Then there is his mom, who feels for her son. "Woe is me, my mother, that thou hast borne a man of strife and contention to the whole earth!" Jeremiah speaks of widows being increased above the sand of the seas, and doubtless, his dear mother was one of them.

Jeremiah wants his mom to understand just how hard it is to be a prophet of God. He refers to it as "the awfulness of his calling as a vessel of God's truth" and that he had found that he had been raised up "not to send peace on earth." Mentally are you ready to be a prophet and carry a prophetic staff?

Imagine being his mom and not understanding this how-to bring condolence to your son's sorrowing heart, seeing he was divinely forbidden to take a wife to weep with him as he wept *(Jeremiah 16:2)*. Once again, as you explore your relationship with God. You are just as different as any other prophet.

Jeremiah provides us, today's prophets, insight into how to handle being uniquely un-normal. He did struggle with life, anxious thoughts, and fears; Jeremiah displays this throughout his life. Jeremiah found his way, and you will also. Again this book is focused on the mental edge, the mentality of walking with a prophetic staff today. The walk away from yourself normal is real and a fact in the prophetic. Your struggle will be authentic, also.

Let me help you adjust to the loss of normalcy in your life as you now start to understand the value of the process that your prophetic staff has placed on your life. Allow these three points to be guideposts in your life, as what was normal is no more.

1. You must know that God's calling is authentic and your life assignment.

Jeremiah 1:5, "God tells Jeremiah, he knew him before he was in his mom's womb." Reminiscent of Moses, Jeremiah questions his ability to live up to God's appointed position. God assures Jeremiah that he is the man for the task.

Amid lonely times and our trying periods of ministry, we see Jeremiah knew these words of God. They were his points of comfort. Jeremiah's prophetic office was not a charity. It wasn't just handed to him. God chose and ordained him. Despite what was happening, he knew God cared for him. Prophet and Seers, we must do the same and know what to do.

Many of us, like Jeremiah, have been called before birth. In Ephesians 1:4–6, God has destined us for His adoption as His children through Jesus Christ. This is according to the good pleasure of God Himself and His freely bestowed grace on us, His Beloved."

God has chosen us and appointed us to be His prophets. Remember this the next time someone gets brand new with you. There are provisions with the calling of God. Jeremiah was promised that he would be delivered from his enemies, and God did just that. Therefore, I boldly share that God will pay you for what you have been through or are going through. Apply this to those struggling with the concept of a Prophetic Staff.

The gift of singleness can be a blessing and a burden. What about when it feels like it is far too much to bear? We wait on God despite what seems to be overwhelming. Imagine wanting to know someone intimately. We have prophets going through this and more today. We can't forget that God does know us intimately and longs for our affection.

David, in *Psalm 68:6,* says that the Lord cares for us and *"makes a home for the lonely."* The walk with a prophetic staff will be lonely sometimes. In Hebrews 13:5, we are reminded that this same loving God will never leave us, nor will He forsake us either.

2. Trust God's assignment

To know the truth is one thing, but to act upon it is quite another. In life, questions will remain unanswered in this sea of loneliness: If God truly loved me, could He not at least provide one or two close friends? If God loved me, couldn't He eliminate some of the financial burdens?

Imagine the questions that Jeremiah must have asked during his time of ministry. "Why does the pain I feel unceasing? Do you feel your wound is incurable? Prophet, what part of you do you feel refuses to be healed? Have you, like Jeremiah, compared yourself to a deceitful brook? In *Jeremiah 15:18,* he asks himself as we do, is God faithful? Can he depend on the word of God? Where is God when one of His prophets needs relief? You will doubt yourself as you carry a prophetic staff and get criticized.

Trusting God despite the circumstances requires your personal and intimate meditation upon His promises and reflection upon His past actions. Like many of us, Jeremiah questioned God's love and ability to provide. Our confidence is in God's love for us. That says it all. We simply need to look to God. Reflect on what He has done in our lives.

Despite times of loneliness and the knowledge that he would always be single, in *Jeremiah 16:1–9,* Jeremiah confidently declares the Word of God. He identifies God as his strength and fortress. In *Jeremiah 16:19,* we see that He continues with his praise of God. He knows who he is. He trusts God, and places hope in Him to be blessed. He is in a world of couples, but he is alone *(Jeremiah 17:7).*

Reread this. Let us see ourselves here as we carry the Prophetic Staff. We are learning now more about God and ourselves. My prayer is that you start to feel confident about who you are and how you have been called. Trust in the fact that what was normal is different now.

3. God's perspective and the prophet's prayer

Prophet, you must become attuned to possessing God's perspective. This is key to trusting in the Lord; this is not always easy. As you walk and minister with your staff, ensure that you read how Jeremiah wrestled with life and his role as a prophet. There is no doubt about this. We also see that he remained faithful to God. What was enlighting was that Jeremiah recognized that his suffering and the judgment upon the people of Judah both were temporary. "The prophet does not see the world from the point of view of politics; they are a person who sees the world from the point of view God has. The prophet sees the world through the eyes of God." This is plain and simple.

Jeremiah had a deposited experience, so he understood the work of God. Learn what he learned; he looks at the eternal rather than what he knew was temporary. A vital issue with prophets and loneliness is that it is so easy to lose sight of why God has called you as a prophet.

God has a purpose for how He appoints us. He has a purpose for who will carry a staff and who will not.

Prophet, ongoing communion with the Lord is essential to maintaining God's perspective on your life. Prayer serves as a vehicle for wisdom. Prayer will give clarification from God as we take time to listen. In *Jeremiah 32:25,* spend time as you will, understanding the prophetic staff.

You will attempt to unearth your and his confusion. He learns how to speak God's word upon himself. Jeremiah speaks understanding. His prayer life demonstrates the intimacy he has with God. Jeremiah learned how to speak freely to God concerning his issues. He demonstrates an established relationship with God. I cannot stress enough why your relationship with God is so critical as you carry a prophetic staff.

We have challenged our intellect in the first two chapters. I advise you to go back and reread them if you struggle to see the concept of being a prophet with a staff. What does it mean to you, and how will you handle this type of assignment from God? Are you up to the task, and are you strong enough mentally to move forward? The reality is that God is calling us now, and we have to trust Him and His plan for our lives.

Those in our lives we lose, we count it joy as we move forward in the Mantle of Moses and other great prophets. There is a reality here that we must acknowledge: God is calling our lives into order via *The Prophetic Staff.*

CHAPTER 3

CALLING THE PROPHET'S LIFE TO ORDER VIA THE PROPHETIC STAFF

There is a special anointing on a prophet's life when God calls the prophet's life to order. This is true for those assigned to walk with the staff. There is a humbling in the prophet who will realize and experience the true essence of walking with a prophetic staff. You are not better than anyone, but you are different than many you will encounter; as we look in the prophetic ministry, we see that not every prophet has their life called to order by God.

When God calls a prophet's life to order, that prophet will experience an uninterrupted relationship of God's Glory upon their life. You will live a life of God's realized glory in your finances, health, and debt; trouble will pass you by or not affect you. This is a special connection with God that you will experience.

You will see the blessings of God where you go, and you will cause others connected to you to walk in the blessings of God because you are connected to His blessings. Divine Order for the prophet is all about the moving of the Holy Spirit, and the prophet is focused enough to hear His voice and flexible enough to go with the flow of what God is doing.

Let's explore that you have been called to walk with a prophetic staff. The calling had you feeling like a novice prophet. You did not know what to do. How does this happen, and how do you handle this? What and why does not every prophet of God experience the benefits of calling your life into order?

Could there be reasons why every prophet does not experience this, yet it is available to every prophet? The answer we are looking for is yes, the anointing is available to every prophet, but we must be wise in how we throw the concept of having our lives called to order via our prophetic staff.

The word of God is a light unto us as prophets and a path for us to get understanding. Let's look at *Deuteronomy 28*. This provides us the absolute proof of promised blessings. Blessings for the prophet that are not to be debated, nor can they be ignored or denied.

These blessings are for you, prophet, and the reason some prophets have God call their life to order and others do not is found in the revelation of *Deuteronomy 28*.

All prophets who read this should spend quality time here and keep reading until you get this concept. God wants to bless His prophets whether you have a prophetic staff. Again, I want you to have the mentality of a seasoned mature, and confident prophet.

You carry a prophetic staff; unless you are mentally ready, you will only fool yourself by carrying the staff. This is the mentality of walking with a prophetic staff in this now generation. You must be ready.

Deuteronomy 28, read the first ten verses. *We are to hearken diligently unto the voice of the Lord. We are to observe and do all His commandments. God will set thee on high above all nations of the earth, and we shall see and experience blessings.* I am talking about blessings that shall overtake us. We must know the voice of God.

There are some critical keys the prophet must understand and be willing to represent. When I harken, I understand that I submit, which brings me to the point that the prophet must believe. The ability to believe determines the prophet's ability to receive the blessings of God. The prophet must be able to believe certain things about themselves.

I must say here; we should not fool ourselves. This must start with the prophet's mind, understanding that words are the seeds of life that will come forth because of what you choose to believe or not believe. This includes the establishment of yourself as a prophet who carries a staff.

If you believe you should not be sick or broken, you will receive words supporting that belief system. You will receive the Word of God. You will demonstrate a Spiritual Conviction, a drive that you harken to the words, "It shall come to pass." Do you believe that God has called you to walk with the assignment of the Prophetic Staff?

Do you believe it or not? Answer the question now for yourself. The Apostle Paul says I can do everything through Christ that strengthens me. So that means that if I line up with His word and work, my ministry, then it will work. But a key Word that needs to be looked at is "diligently." When diligent, we allow the conviction to connect with our focus and get things done. Will you diligently develop your relationship with God and be willing to learn more about your assignment to carry a prophetic staff?

The focus moves us to a level of learning how to prioritize God's work and business to the point that when God calls on a prophet, the prophet hears God and follows through. The storms of life around the prophet do not affect the clear vision of the prophet. Who is this prophet, what does this prophet know, and what is the driving force behind the prophet? Now as you carry a prophetic staff, these are questions you must answer.

This prophet is the prophet who is committed to the task God has given them. This prophet is the prophet of God, who is not concerned with pleasing people, playing politics, or building social based relationships. This is the prophet God calls his or her life into divine order because the prophet's actions and work support God's word of "it shall come to pass." You are the prophet who will carry a staff and work the staff for the glory of God.

Deuteronomy 28 says, "Blessed in the city, blessed in the field. Blessed be the body's fruit, your ground is blessed, and your animals are blessed, with increase followed by even more blessings." This only happens when your focus is on God, and you operate in a diligent manner.

When you focus and work diligently, God will bless you anywhere you're at, and He will move you anywhere, and He will bless you. Prophet, wherever God sends you is what your assignment is. God can send you to any nation, any state, and you will experience His blessings. What am I saying to you? I am saying that God will bless you as you walk into the work of carrying a prophetic staff.

The issue today of the Joshua Generation prophet is that many prophets and prophetic people have stopped expecting God's blessings, and to be blunt, they have given up. We all know examples of this whether we speak it publicly or not.

Maybe it's because man has said no. Maybe because there is no focus on God's word, or maybe it's because someone has given us a title and they had no clue, and we took it, and we don't either. This is why I am sharing with you on the prophetic staff. Six years of experience since I wrote the initial Prophetic Staff book has dictated a need for us all to prepare ourselves mentally.

While we have no time to waste, we must never stop learning. If the Word of God says that it shall come to pass, we need to be able to speak it upon ourselves and know that it shall come to pass.

Deuteronomy 28 again speaks of our blessings, and if we harken to God, He will handle our haters. God will anoint us with the anointing of prosperity as He fills our storehouses, and where ever we lay our hands, the intended purposes of God will come to pass.

There are far too many discouraged prophets who are operating in the spirit of hopelessness. The reasons are as diverse as the prophetic gifts themselves. The bottom line is that when there is a lack of diligence and unbelief, it affects your receiving from God. This is a core reason why prophets doubt themselves in specialized giftings such as walking with a prophetic staff.

Acts 1:18 says that God has given us power, and we do not use it. Why are we praying for God to give us power over what He has already blessed us? We will not use it because we do not know or realize we have it. The Word of God has given you power, and we are lost to the fact, and the utilization of it is a mystery.

The word says, "If thou shall harken diligently, not halfhearted, it shall come to pass." Prophet, God calls your life into order; how He does it is on us. This is clearly on us, not the devil, not your in-laws, or another prophet. Hebrews 11 says that God is the rewarder of those who will diligently seek Him. Remember, in the previous chapters, we talked about this being personal.

The prophet of all the 5-fold ministry gifts must diligently seek God. You are the one to whom God has given the assignment to carry a staff. Why are and when are things going slow to maybe nothing? What is going on?

The word is to remain a diligent prophet. Stay diligent. When there is no diligence, there is no reward. Sadly, there are far too many prophets listening to demonic voices that are prolonging and stalling their progress and simply making them not like themselves.

Welcome to spiritual warfare as we fight. According to *2 Corinthians 10:4, the weapons of our warfare are not carnal; they are simply for the mighty work of God as strongholds are pulled down.*

The ministry of torment is real as we apply faith because, without faith, our works are dead. This is the foundation of diligence as we do it, move forth, focus on God, and now He puts order in our life. The foundation of diligence makes us check on our lives and demonstrate life's checks and balances according to the Word of God.

When you, prophet, address and speak to your issues, you set yourself up for God to order your life with His divine order. This is how you simply become a force for God as you are now in alignment with God. Yes, there is a place for you today as you walk with your prophetic staff.

Your walking with the prophetic staff puts you in alignment with the order of God. Alignment and order walk hand in hand. Let's look at the fact that God's order brings clarity. To illustrate, we can look at the prophet's finances as an example.

When we give to God, we are out of alignment if we are giving emotionally. You give, and then you talk about it, brag about it, or want people to know you're a giver, so you give and alert the whole circle you run in.

Emotional giving: To give and get the blessings of God upon your seed, you must give and exercise discipline. The exact process must be given to your walk with the prophetic staff. Give your best to God, and He will give you His blessings. The exercise of discipline is a trademark of God. Discipline is what a disciple or prophet exercises in every area of their life.

God will only call your financial life to order when you show the necessary discipline in your giving as you observe God's laws on finance. This now positions you for the resources of God's blessings you have never imagined.

God will call your prophetic ministry to order when you exercise the discipline that will harken to His word. God will not call us to order unless we show Him that we will harken to His word. We will line up and surrender to Him. Allow your diligence and commitment to overtake you and run you down in the form of blessings.

Know that trouble is a magnet for development, especially in the life of the prophet. Some prophets do not surrender to Him, proclaim that trouble is all around them, and somehow do not realize that they are cursed because of their dysfunctionality. When you have had enough trouble, you will allow yourself to submit, and God will call your life into order. This is a reason why we see prophets who are stressed and gifted, and yet nothing is happening for God's purposes.

Drama disappears, trouble ceases, and health improves as the blessings of God overtake you literally, and you walk in the order of God. When God orders your life, you now enter the season that you will move away from that defeated mentality and victimization and intimation, and most of all, you enter into a new reality.

CHAPTER 4

MY STAFF, NO MORE DISRESPECT OF GOD'S PROPHET

God uses men and women. He has different purposes. We also know God has delegated His people's needs to different ministries. He knows what is paramount. The prophetic is one such ministry. The prophetic is paramount.

The prophetic, because it is high profile, always seems to catch its fair share of criticism, unbelief, and downright disrespect. There can be many reasons, such as prior upbringing, hurt or jealousy, or simply the will of God, that someone is not called to be a prophet. We know there are people who do not accept us for the role of leadership, perhaps because they disagree with how the prophetic ministry works or just having the belief they can do a better job.

The reality is many talks against and about the prophet and what a dangerous mistake they make when they do so. I am saying this as many may talk more about you because you now walk with a staff. They will not understand, or maybe they will not accept it.

Whatever the case, be advised that you are God's prophet, and He has directed you to carry a staff. May I suggest *2 Kings 1:1-17*?

Ahaziah and Elijah simply have a falling out. As you read the first 17 verses, you will see a unique situation that should encourage you. We have King Ahaziah seeking out a god that shows disrespect for the God of Elijah.

Elijah checks him and tells him that he will not leave his bed and will die for his misdeeds. Elijah goes his way and runs into messengers of Ahaziah and tells them basically the same thing, and sends them back to Ahaziah. The King is upset and wants to know who sent his messages back. They describe Elijah, and now King Ahaziah sends 50 men to bring Elijah back.

Can you imagine Elijah sitting on a hill and he speaks to the Captain of the men and tells him very pointedly to leave him alone? He speaks that if he is indeed a prophet, fire will come down from the sky and destroy him and his men.

The disrespect of Elijah is real, as the Captain ignored his words. This was what cost the Captain his life and his 50 men. We are stunned to see this happen again; now, one hundred and two men are dead as they have failed in their effort to intimidate Elijah.

Now the third group of men comes to Elijah. This time the Captain speaks to Elijah with respect, and he lives, and Elijah goes with him to see the King. The King still dies as the prophet said he would. Notice this about Elijah as he spoke and handled himself with confidence, knowing that God had his back.

God has called you to carry a prophetic staff. There is a reason God has chosen you. You want to know why, go to God and allow Him to reveal His purpose and plan for your life. This is what is important. There will always be those who choose to disrespect; this is what they do. This is what they are good at. The reality is that we also benefit from them as it pushes us closer to God.

God is serious about your standing with Him. He will protect you as He protected Elijah. Your calling to walk with a prophetic staff is a big deal. This will distinguish you, spur conversation, and people will wonder and want to know more and why.

You now have the responsibility to become not just a prophet but an ambassador for God as you explain the ministry of the staff. There is a reality that we must know and embrace God will protect His prophets, and He will deal with the disrespect of them, that He has called to the work of the prophetic.

Notice *Psalm 105:14-15* as the word speaks of The Nation Israel and Her Prophets. Our God speaks to us in His Word. Now man is to do us wrong, including kings and leaders on all levels in the Body of Christ today. Many who have attempted to go the way of the king did not prosper as the anointing of God was untouched upon our lives prophet.

We must know that God will deal with us, and we must know that He knows and has invested in us. There is a vast difference between dealing with a godly prophet and an ungodly prophet. Many would be wise to be careful and not raise a hand or voice against a true man of God.

There are biblical examples and some true-life illustrations of God's dealing with those who did His prophets harm. God is still true to His Word. Touch not; we are His; He has assigned us. Prophet, use your staff, work the work of your calling, and be glad and excited.

Look at examples of those who disrespected God's prophets. Ahab, an exceedingly wicked king, died by way of prophetic utterance. He is struck by an arrow and bleeds to death. Ahaziah did not die in battle as his dad Ahab did. He falls out of his window and plunges to the ground.

Those of you who are military or have served know the value of a soldier by several factors. Submission is one of the most important factors. When soldiers refuses to obey orders, they become repulsive to the noncommissioned officer or commissioned officer who is put in charge of them. You will always see a lack of information flow to this type of soldier.

Soldiers are intentionally kept in the dark by command many times for mission security. So we see soldiers working with only partial information. Submission is simply so critical to an army of humans on any battlefield.

I say this as we see soldiers here who died by following orders. They did now know who Elijah was. Even if they had heard of him, they did not know what he carried. Had they known, they probably would have refused to go and die blindly because someone wanted to dominate God's prophet.

The opposite of this is your status as a soldier in the army of the Lord. You are a prophet. Prophet, you are a soldier; the difference is that you have been given the knowledge of God and His wisdom to know how to handle and respect authority and deal with disrespect to your spiritual heritage. You have it now; others may not, but you must handle yourself with dignity and character.

God does have a special place in His heart for His prophets. But many of us simply refuse to go through the process of His validation, which leads us to not be like Elijah in the way we handle ourselves. This is a true fact, and even within our ranks, we find disrespect and disgrace among our ranks.

Ask yourself, if I am indeed a prophet, why am I experiencing disrespect? Why do I not have a clue on how to deal with it? Disrespect is a primary characteristic of people in the end times. In *Isaiah 3:5* this end time reference of people being disrespected, people who hold positions of honor, and yet we see the indignity of dishonor upon their lives. *2 Timothy 3:1-4* says we are to be lovers of ourselves. To put it simply, we are, as scripture says, disobedient, unthankful, unloving, unforgiving, and, yes, unholy.

Even as we casually read the Word of God, we see that disrespect of a prophet is not taken lightly by God.

In *Numbers 12:9-10* when Miriam and Aaron spoke against Moses, Miriam was plagued with leprosy, and Aaron was significantly humbled. In *Numbers 21:5-6,* when the people of Israel spoke against God and Moses, God sent fiery serpents to chastise them for their sin. In *Numbers 16:2-3* when Korah and over 250 others spoke against Moses and Aaron, we see here that God allowed the earth to swallow Korah and the others up. In *2 Kings 2:22-23* when children mocked God's man, Elisha, God allowed two she bears to destroy 42 mockers.

As you see those references, did you notice that David would not go against King Saul, even though he did know the King did wrong? David's had in his heart, "LORD forbid that I, David, should stretch forth mine hand against the LORD'S anointed: ..." Why was this, and Saul was not even a prophet?

In *I Samuel 26:11,* we should follow David's lead and allow leaders to counsel leaders, as he knows it was not good to expose God's man, speaking of Saul then. This includes against the prophet of God or even leaders of the local church. So when I speak that people will speak against you as you carry a prophetic staff, know that you are chosen by God.

Prophet, please understand that you will not destroy disrespect. It abounds because of woeful ignorance of the Bible. Do you agree with me that we have a great number of people that lack a healthy fear of God? While we see how God feels about relationships, we don't seem to be able to emphasize the love for God and love for all people.

Mutual respect is a standard of love; it is fundamental to good relationships. It would be very wise for you to consider building the right relationships moving forth. Your ability to be effective with your staff will not dictate you to be arrogant because you carry a prophetic staff. Go back and reread the previous chapters; we are working on your mentality so you can represent God with honor.

This is key to having respect for what is important and holy to God, even when we don't understand the gifts or what God is doing through our lives. God's prophets are important to Him, whether some of us choose to acknowledge it or not.

This is a great opportunity to point out some disrespectful issues that you may face as a prophet in general, whether you have a staff or not. Let's look at disrespectful issues that most prophets seem to notice during a prophetic service, especially when they may be ministering or attending a service.

Many people intentionally do things to not have the prophet reveal thing things. They want the prophet to get irritated and upset and hope the prophet will not reveal their sin. This is why a prophet's focus is so critical. Let's look at some challenges we see in Prophetic Ministry that are disrespectful.

1.Talking during service. This will vary from culture to culture. Some seem to see no disrespect and will hold a conversation to get the prophet's attention, or you want to get attention off of God and His prophetic mouthpiece.

So this type of person will allow themselves to be the enemy pawn because of their lack of understanding of the prophetic. These can also be the person who is chewing gum and smacking and using the meeting as a social event. The bottom line is this is disrespect.

2.Texting or surfing the web or answering a ringing phone during service. Yes, there are emergency situations, and a leader's responsibility may dictate to have a phone on. If it is necessary, then it is necessary to have the phone on at no volume or vibrate without noise.

Other prophets and people who answer the phone right in church are past disrespectful, and you really should assess why you are there in the first place. This is so disrespectful, and now consider how you may be received as you minister with your staff.

3. Sleeping or snoring during a service. Prophets, if available, ask the ushers or attendants to assist that person, even if it means leaving the service. They clearly are not interested in being in the service. They need rest that they have not gotten. They are pawns to get attention, and your focus is broken, do not fall for it. Speak directly and with your authority.

4. Constantly getting up and leaving the auditorium, presumably to use the restroom or walking out of a service early, espe-

cially during a prayer or at offering time. Why are your bile's and your bladder always like clockwork having to be utilized?

We also see mothers and adults allowing babies to cry incessantly in the service and allowing their child to crawl or run around the church, and sit there and will not discipline the child. There are even times that the child will be allowed to walk around the speaker who is ministering and be a distraction. This is not cute; this is disrespectful, and what's amazing is the number of people who get offended when asked to attend to their child.

5. Once in the service, it is not your responsibility to nor are you commissioned to start a prayer circle or a prayer meeting in the corner during the meeting while the prophet is praying and ministering to the people. What makes you think that God has called you to override His servant, who He is using to minister to His people?

You now become a spectacle, and despite your claims of the Holy Ghost, you are so far out of order that you are lost within yourself and not God. Those who do this do not like to be exposed because they mainly play off someone else's anointing, and they have not been in the presence of God because they don't understand order by their disrespectful actions. You also have a friend called the parking lot prophet, and sometimes they're one in the same.

There is a reality here, and much of the issue is that many who confront the prophets directly and indirectly with disrespectful behavior don't want to live right themselves. People who are constantly on a slander attack against the prophets should likewise be held to the standards of discipline found in *Matthew 18*. A perpetual gossiping tongue in the fellowship of the Body of Christ or a church creates an atmosphere of confusion, and that individual proves to be a messenger of Satan.

When we belittle one of God's ministries, we do much damage. Murmuring against God's prophets is sin, and sin can only do harm to one's life. Murmuring about prophets working for Christ puts one in a position of judging another, in this case, prophets. *(Mat. 7:1)*. This is now what you or I do; it is the Holy Spirit's job, in most situations, not ours.

Murmuring prophets will always sow seeds of discord. Most of the time, this behavior will only hinder, not build, your ministry *(Proverbs 6:16-19)*. Speaking against the prophets, or other God-appointed leaders, hinders the Holy Spirit of God from working in one's life and very quickly could bring the wrath of God on the violators.

Aaron and Hur knew about the principle of helping. This should be followed to help any man or woman of God and would be encouraged today. Can you see how they both noticed Moses' arms were up as he directed the battle against Israel?

When Moses was tired and could not lift up his arms, the battle was in the enemy's favor. Aaron and Hur ensured Moses' arms were held high on each side. This put them in a position to get the victory. Yes, know that they physically held up their leader's arms.

If more people realized that honoring God's servants, such as prophets, is honoring God and His work, more spiritual battles would be won, and more prophets of relevance would emerge. Lift up your leader's arms. Do not force them down, especially by your disrespect or the "I have a better way!"

God will not dispute Himself with you having a better way to attempt to circumvent your leadership to prove something to yourself or others whom you may try to impress. "If you don't have anything good to say, don't say anything!" When you encounter a prophet with a gift you are unfamiliar with or have no knowledge of, do yourself a favor. Shut your mouth, pray, and seek knowledge.

Furthermore, God made every human being *"in the image of God" (Genesis 1:27)*. Every prophet of God has a destiny, and you do not know who will be, who to you tomorrow in the Body of Christ. That's why every human being deserves to be treated with dignity and respect.

This is why this book is dedicated to all prophets, whether you carry a prophetic staff or not. You carry His anointing, which makes you just as special as the prophet who carries a prophetic staff or a prophet who specializes in revival or both.

Become the best version of yourself; that's what is important. The mentality I want to convey for those who carry a staff is critical, and for those who are gifted and may not carry a staff, understand it is still critical.

CHAPTER 5

MY STAFF AND PROPHETIC INFLUENCE

As a prophet, people will see you, and your mere presence will intimidate them because of your influence. The prophetic staff you carry will multiply that. People do not realize that everything that lives changes eventually. This includes us prophets. For the prophet, we must recognize that our change is a direct reflection of God living in us.

We define influence as the effect on the behavior and character of an individual. Prophetic influence causes a prophet to act on the fact that they are a prophet, and their actions reflect just that. Prophetic influence is effective in change. This is why your staff is important, and your staff represents change for any on how they see and receive the prophet of this now generation. You are important.

This is why prophets are agents of change. You bring change, and your staff yells change for so many. God has and may call you to a region, a country, or a specific place, and you bring the change that God wants. Prophetic influence now becomes the impact that the prophet must operate within the eyes of His people. This is why your staff is not for you to model with. Your staff is a tool of God. Most who will see you will not be familiar with your staff and how God may choose to use it.

Prophets listen closely; you can't control how people see you. Because you can't control that, you need God to give you the influence in their eyes to get it done. Your influence, prophetic influence, is for the Glory of God. Prophet, we need to remember that your individual prophetic influence is proportional to your personal authority and status as an individual prophet. The way you choose to handle yourself with your staff is critical.

Does the room change when you walk in, or does the atmosphere shift? Can you speak with someone and change what manifests? There is a reality of our mentalities within the prophetic that we must respect and practice. We must know who we are, or we have no influence because of no impact. Every prophet must evaluate how many things they do without prophetic influence.

Question? #1 How many of us as prophets are unsure of our calling, and do you know it affects your influence?

Question #2 How many of us don't feel we are effective as prophets? Rest assured, your carrying a prophetic staff will test you to your very depths.

One thing that prophets must realize is that we have to learn how to pray for prophetic influence in the eyes of those we are sent to serve. What I am saying is that the prophet can seek God to be effective for the will of God to be done.

God will often create a crisis or trouble as He did for Joshua to change the opinion of people who knew Joshua. God wanted the people to see him differently. The prophet gains influence by dealing with pressure. I am trying to tell you that your staff will generate pressure for you. The staff will put you in a place mentally that if you are not ready, you will be exposed. Do not allow this to happen.

Prophetic influence happened for Joshua and will happen for you, also. People see you prophet by how you conduct yourself and what you say in a crisis, trouble, or chaos, and yes, that is how you operate under pressure. This is what establishes your prophetic influence.

The process of establishing prophetic influence births from the fact that you are doing what God created you to do, and that is to be a prophet. You are His prophet. This will not matter to everyone, as many of us as prophets have found out. This matters to you to whom God has called and to whom you are called to serve on His behalf.

This is why the prophet must be educated on the fact that what happens in the prophetic realm is of little to no concern to those who do not understand or accept it. We see this played out over and over again on social media and in many of our denominational churches. The prophet must guard against opinions not assigned to your mantle.

Prophetic influence provides education upfront and personally in the life of a prophet as to function when, where, and how God speaks to His prophet. So many of us do not get this as we are influenced by those who view us and form opinions. This influence is short-lived at best because they are external and not internal.

In *Ephesians 1:18,* the great Apostle Paul prays that the eyes of our understanding are enlightened, and this is needed and necessary to help us understand our purpose. Influence starts within, so as Apostle Paul prays, we see this played out in our lives. Notice here it begins within, and it is revealed in our lives. Your carrying a staff is what it is; it is the will of God.

Too many of us feel that we are fake prophets and are not living in our purpose. The eyes of understanding are opened as the spirit of understanding is free to move within our lives. I decree this upon your life as you read this.

Joshua was enlightened before he went before the people as their new leader. God deals with him first. Notice the internal action versus the external. God will deal with you on the inside before we see it on the outside.

This is why there is a war going on inside as you have wrestled with your choice to carry a staff. In *Joshua Ch. 1,* God shows us the internal as he speaks to Joshua and tells him to be strong and be of good courage. Joshua had to know who he was now at this time in his life. The same is true for you now.

God convinced Joshua, but has He convinced you, prophet? Are you ready to walk into your calling, thoroughly convinced that you are called? Do you know your gift? Do you know your purpose? Do you know you are in the right place? Do you know before anyone else knows?

Are you ready for prophetic influence or not? What's funny is the fact that the people wanted Moses, and God has taken him, and we see again in Joshua Ch. 1 that God speaks to him and tells him as He was with Moses, He will be that way with him. The people will see him differently, and his influence will greatly increase. Can you trust that for your life?

Prophets, the reality of an increase in prophetic influence means a total increase. Your harvest, responsibilities, enemies, and pressure are increased. Can you handle the increase that so many of us seek? This is what you can expect as you minister with your prophetic staff.

This is where prophets should make a personal note to themselves. Ask yourself, do you need help with your present responsibilities across the board? What are you dealing with that is keeping you stuck? Realize and be honest with yourself that you need some work before you seek additional prophetic influence.

This is what happens so much that it is not even funny. A prophet works hard to be ordained and now seeks prophetic influence. The things the prophet was doing, they do no more. They develop a sense of unspoken pride that reflects in their life. Your anointed and appointed, but you must stay humble.

What was hidden is now on full display, and you seek prophetic influence when your birthing is still in process. The sad reality of trying to do something you are ill-equipped to do is realized. You now are exposed prophet.

Prophetic influence exposes you to the areas you are untrained or need training. The simple reason is the increase in every area of your life, and if you are not ready for it, you will be exposed. I say again, for the third time, you will be exposed.

We see prophets broadly decree and make declarations and through all that, we fail to adequately represent the assignment we are given. People are watching us whether they tell us or not. We are targets and while the understanding of our craft is not always understood, that is simply no excuse for us as we operate in prophetic influence.

Joshua shows us about being in a state of increase. The next level of influence demands that we are prepared to step into an arena we have never been in before. This means we have to be willing to change.

We cannot assume the mantle of prophetic influence and think that we will not change. We will change. The staff you walk with will change you. How you handle your staff will change you. I will discuss this in a later chapter on how you should handle your staff.

Notice that Joshua changed, and we will also. Prophetic influence affects the behavior of those to whom the prophet is sent and to those to whom the prophet serves. Prophetic influence is bigger than the prophet and this is why the prophet must realize that they are not the centerpiece; the will of God is still the most important thing to experience.

As prophets, our mandate is to pour into a person, group, or situation for the purpose of change. Remember, we are the agents of change. We must recognize the assignment and what God is calling for us to do.

Luke 2:52 says that Jesus increased in wisdom and stature. This is important for the prophet to see and develop from. The issue of influence increasing is seen here in the New Testament from Jesus Himself as an example for the now-generation prophet.

As we see Jesus and His influence increased, we should learn that our tolerance increases to certain things we encounter. The prophet's tolerance matches their influence. This is why you do not want to live anyone's life but your own. You have been chosen to carry the prophetic staff and your ability to do that is vital to God's purpose for your life.

Prophet, your tolerance is built to the level of influence you walk in. This is why when people put their mouths on you, it will roll off your back, and you will remain focused. Your focus as a prophet who carries a staff may not allow for a tolerance for the amount of pressure your brother or sister may be under. That's between them and God; know when it is and is not your assignment.

To those prophets who have been scandalized and had your name drugged through the mud at your expense of being processed, learn who can grow with and who cannot grow with. Look to see those in your life who are uncomfortable with your growth. This includes you as you carry the prophetic staff.

Watch as they reveal themselves, and you will now know who can handle the influence God has given you and who cannot. Why is this critical, because as they reveal themselves, it's the sign that one of you has to separate from the other. Their season in your circle has ended as God has shown you they can't handle your increased prophetic influence. You must trust God that He knows what He is doing in your life.

Those of you who want God to increase your influence understand that your hunger is an indication of your future prophetic influence. One of the hardest lessons we learn as prophets is that we have to separate from the group plan and understand that God created and gifted you for you and you only.

Prophets who are untrainable and unteachable will not be able to walk with you as you increase in influence prophetically. We should demand that the prophetic community as a whole should not pull them where they don't want to go. The reality is that this has to stop, and we can't be allowed to disrespect the prophetic gift anymore.

Your hunger has opened the door for you to walk into a higher level of prophetic influence, and you have to accept and trust God in His plan for your life. The prophet must know to whom they are assigned and understand that this can very well include those who have betrayed and disrespected your mantle. Now here you show up with your prophetic staff, and the way you deal with how they react to you is important.

Every prophetic leader and prophet in our history has had people betray, hurt, embarrassed, or misrepresented them to the public. You will need to be able to overcome this. They have left our charge. They have gone their way, and now that they see the increase of influence upon your life. Can you handle them as they seek to return?

This happens time and time again. This will happen to you also as you handle yourself the correct way. Can you see yourself with your prophetic staff, a simple piece of wood and tool of God? Now they seek to model themselves after your mantle because of how you handled yourself, and that was with class, I pray.

Their immaturity has faded, and the question now is being able to handle the influence God has given you because you are likely to have your influence maintained with people or even prophets you may not even like or trust, yet this is whom God has given you.

Are you big enough and mature enough to handle this type of situation of dealing with a prodigal prophet? A prodigal prophet whom God has assigned to you, and now you are expected to be mature enough because of your increased prophetic influence.

Prophetic influence has placed you in a place you have never been in, but you trust God anyway. You must grow as a prophetic voice who trusts God. The prophet that will not increase because your irritation is fueled by the past faults and issues of others. Prophet, the past will cause you to lose your influence in the now day season. Walk away from your issues, learn from them and go forth.

A great part of the prophet's life is spent dealing with people who are difficult, small-minded, and generally not walking in a level of faith that is mandated by the prophetic call. With this being a known fact, growth for the prophet is critical. Your carrying a prophetic staff will elevate you to this position as you will be in the bullseye of difficult people.

God is calling us to grow in the midst of things that make simply no sense. What the prophet learns is quite simple and yet extremely complex to learn. Joseph gives us an example to follow and embrace as a Seer.

The fact is that people and prophets do change. Matter of fact we see that Joseph changed as he grew in his walk with God. The changing of people, especially prophets, is a fact. The fact is that it does not change that I am a leader. They are given the option to grow just like any of us. While some mistakes were made, some things were said, and some things were done.

Joseph said what was meant for bad is now been turned around by God. This is learning how to live and walk with prophetic influence. What the prophet of today needs to learn is that people, whether they are with you or not, do not change your destiny. Understanding the fact that people don't change your destiny, but they can help enlarge your influence is priceless.

This is why God will make it necessary for you to forgive, so as a prophet of God, you can work through what God needs you to. How many of us, as prophets today, are looking to grow in prophetic influence, and we can't because we are simply too petty?

How many of us can God trust with more, and how many of us can God not trust at this time in our prophetic walks? Do you understand that you have been trusted with more? You carry a prophetic staff, and it is drawing attention. Can you handle the change it brings to your life? Remember you said God told you to carry a prophetic staff. Your life will change when you understand this concept.

To the prophets who seek prophetic influence and God is sending back prophets or even people who caused you to experience betrayal, shame, irritation, and even frustration because of their actions, or if everyone walked away, be advised of the example of Joseph. Your prophetic influence is conditional on whether you are ready for it or not.

In *1 Samuel 14:24-30*, we see that Jonathan demonstrates the principle of the now-day prophet receiving influence. The prophet has to be fed. The scripture says that he dipped his rod into the honey and he ate. Because he ate, his eyes were enlightened. The others were afraid and did not eat. Feeding is a basic need as a prophet's influence proves that your ability to grow is directly related to your ability to be fed.

Prophets, you can be intimidated by man and not get the needed nourishment for your assignment. We see this so often happening today. We want to walk in a level we are unprepared for. We see, and we want. When we learn to move in faith, enlightenment comes upon us, and that opens the door for preparation to the greater. We get a taste of it, and now we are exposed to it.

Joshua got a taste of being a leader, and now we see Jonathan get a taste, and he becomes a leader. The lesson here is that when an emerging prophet gets a taste of real prophetic influence, they become open to growth. Do you really want to be a leader? You may tell me God has called you to walk with a prophetic staff, but are you ready, willing, and able to do that?

Let me state again prophetic influence will open you up to growth. I can assure you that your prophetic staff will give you a taste of prophetic ministry you are probably unfamiliar with. Years ago, when Prophetess Cox and I started carrying our staffs, we blocked out haters, yet they smiled and whispered behind our backs, but we knew who they were. It did not matter. Growth in the prophetic was more important to us. Change in the arena of our life work meant that much to us and still does as you read this. Question, what about you?

My assignment with this book is to challenge you to grow mentally; I stress this again. The key to growing is opening up your opportunity to grow in what God has given you. This is the case with the *Prophetic Staff* and understanding *The Prophetic Influence of the Staff.* Chapter 6 is going to give you some basic groundwork traits that you need to be aware of and master. My goal is for you and I to be successful as we walk with and minister with our prophetic staff. Once again, this means we become the best version of ourselves.

CHAPTER 6

21 SECRET TRAITS FOR SUCCESSFUL PROPHETS WHO GOD HAS CALLED TO HAVE A PROPHETIC STAFF

John 14 Speaks to the fact that if we believe the works that Jesus did, we shall also do and realize we shall do greater works on top of that. We are the prophets of God. We ask, and Our God is able to do. Yes, we carry great responsibility, which is why in the now generation, we need to look at the traits that make us successful.

Understand that you're a prophet that carries a staff. You are learning the spiritual aspects of the staff, like the positions and what you can and can't do. Prophet, we all have this assurance that the ability of greater works is available, but the difference is that the prophets who are successful share some common traits like the ones I present now.

21 Secret Traits Of Successful Prophets Who Carry Prophetic Staffs

1. The prophet must be ruthlessly in managing their time.

There are 24 hours in a day, but some prophets have more productivity than others and end up achieving their life goals soon. The secret to success is managing your time and learning to shut out distractions, negative thoughts, and negative people so that you can focus on the things that matter. Prioritize your proprieties. Examples like Moses show us clearly. Prophet, your staff should be in a place where you can get it, pray with it, and continually offer it unto God.

2. Real prophets do not peak; they mature and evolve.

As a prophet, your best should always be yet to come. The message behind this is simple, always stay a student. Keep learning. Always grow. Your best days aren't behind you; they're yet to come. Joseph always learned; Samuel always learned. You must study, study and study your staff and how God wants to use you with it. You must be open to revelation as you develop your particular style with the staff and your general overall ministry.

3. Prophetic motivation is needed for yourself.

A successful prophet who carries a staff will not rely on people, accomplishments, or random circumstances to keep them motivated. Prophets will always hit long periods of difficulty, challenges, or even failure.

The only way you'll ever push past those discouraging moments is by keeping yourself motivated and on track to success. Amos, Elijah, and Elisha are examples. Spending time with your leaders and other prophets who carry staff will buffer you from long periods of failure. You will be empowered as you push into God even more as your relationship with Him becomes stronger.

4. High goals are the only goals of focused prophets.

The successful staff carrying prophet isn't just about setting goals; it's about setting the right goals. You may be headed in a direction, but only a Godly relationship will ensure you're going the right way. God knows what's really best for you and your family.

Trust yourself and your prophetic leadership as they guide and encourage you to succeed. Set your goals and then work like it's nobody's business but God's and yours to achieve them. Set goals that challenge you and seek to help other like-minded prophets who are emerging with their gifts, even if they are different than yours.

5. The prophet must increase standards.

Successful prophets who carry staffs know that every time they meet their highest expectations, God will double them. They realize this is how they grow! Never let yourself settle into good when great is available. Recognize your accomplishments, then allow God to double it. Elisha doubled the miracles of Elijah. Look for opportunities to work with your staff. Increase your prayer life and seek God for your particular way to work. This is where your relationship with God grows, and your prophetic influence comes to the forefront.

6. Prophet create a prophetic to do list.

As you carry a staff, embrace the habit of using a prophetic list. A list will help you know what you have accomplished, what you need to finish, and what lies ahead. So make a list. Your prophetic list is for today and tomorrow, and work off that list and nothing else.

Know precisely what you need to be doing today, tomorrow, and next year so that you never stray from the path to a successful staff prophet who is focused. This is why you must have a list of what you must do daily, weekly, or monthly. Figure out what works best for you and do it. Keep your prophetic staff always available, as you may need it for warfare and prayer.

7. Your imperfect action is needed.

Your staff is a challenge. To be a success, you must always be willing to challenge yourself. Your work will never be perfect; you will never be perfect. To meet the challenge of being a successful prophet, know that perfection never comes when you're always making improvements, especially on God's mandate.

If you're faithful, you will see your imperfect work be valuable to the lives of God's people. What's imperfect to a prophet may be just what someone needs for deliverance. This should be every Contemporary Prophet today. Take this as a mentality standard for your personal growth.

8. Know your destructive weakness as you carry a staff.

Successful prophets who carry staffs know how to kill their weakness. Your focus has to be on point. They don't spend their time on tasks they aren't anointed to do. Instead, they outsource and get empowered. Constant improvement is only worth it when you are following God's plan for your life. Successful staff carrying prophets know how to focus on their assigned mission and delegate the rest, especially if God has them in a specific zone. Moses, Elijah, Elijah, and Samuel knew how to do this.

9. Always be sure you kill the negative.

As you carry your staff to be successful prophets, you must manage the negative thoughts, people, and situations. By now, you should have read the previous chapters as we explored how to deal with the negatives. Don't let your thoughts or the comments of others convince you that you won't succeed. God has called you to succeed, and you will. Be a prophet who carries a staff and manages your life. Cut off the negative out of your life, and focus on your next task, accomplishment, or success. Study Moses, Elijah, Elijah, Samuel and others, but do not process the negatives.

10. Get rid of "good enough;" it is not.

You carry your staff; the staff identifies you as a special prophet of excellence and settling for the minimum is a no-go. Let me be clear. Being lazy and having no time to willing devote to your craft is unacceptable. You may be able to get by, but you're hurting so many when God has called you to excellence.

Prophet, do not do this to please others and your constant excuses of why you can't don't matter anymore. Become the type of prophets that whenever you have a problem, you work to fix it. Trust God and stop playing ghost. We, as prophets, are the reflection of God's Word, and if His Word is great, then that's our standard. Learn and maintain the mentality of the Prophetic Staff.

11. Never be afraid of failure with your staff.

To be successful with your staff, you will learn from failure. Failure is your friend and a teacher that God will use to draw you closer to Him. Prophets do not be afraid to get it wrong. Don't let the fear of getting something wrong stop you from getting it right. You will never grow unless YOU FAIL. Prophets get over your fear of it, get past it when it happens, and don't let it keep you from succeeding (Balaam and Jonah). You will not grow until you fail. Despite your efforts to succeed always, you will fail. So fail big and grow.

12. Learn from those who are.

Your ability to be a successful prophet is knowing that God always has someone who has been gifted to excel in certain areas like yours. Remember, you are not the only prophet who will carry a staff. Build relationships and learn from others. Find those who operate in a high level of excellence.

Prophets, instead of responding with disappointment, jealousy, or discouragement, get over your pride and learn from those more proficient in the operation of your area of prophetic excellence. Who is your mentor? And if you don't have one, why? Again this is bigger than you and your pride.

13. Ask for needed help; there is no shame.

You carry a staff, and you should have no use for any pride; if you have not lost yours by now, this is the time to lose it. Questions will arise in your growing as a prophet with a staff. Embrace them and ask questions. You will go farther in your learning by asking questions so you can grow. Pride keeps a lot of prophets on the sideline because they will not ask. When you ask and don't just observe, you accelerate the process. Ensure you seek and do this through an active and seasoned prophet.

14. Honor multiplied is respect.

Successful prophets of all eras understand the word respect. You won't ever develop if you're just a stepping stone for someone else's ascent. This means that you will not grow in an environment where there is no respect. This does not matter who you are or who you feel you are.

Successful prophets who carry staffs know who is around them, who respects and disrespects them. Respect yourself and respect those around you. Do whatever it takes to be successful when it comes to treating others or allowing yourself to be treated.

Anything less than respect for who you are and what you are is less than acceptable. Respect is built on honor, the seed of access, no respect, there is no gift exchange. Respect is critical on your part as you lean of yourself and as you learn of your prophetic staff. You want honor; learn respect.

15. Money and its meaning

To be successful with your staff in this generation will cost you some money. Money to maintain it and money to move it and store it. Let's be honest; we live in a different era than our biblical counterparts. Prophet, you must understand money. Money is a tool and defense. Prophets who understand kingdom principles of money invested into the Kingdom.

Becoming rich and wealthy is a byproduct of money management principles which the Word of God educates us on. Rich people are only rich as long as they don't mismanage their money; no one stays wealthy by spending irresponsibly.

Money is freedom, but recklessness is a path to financial ruin. Successful prophets invest in themselves. You need to invest in the upkeep of your staff. Do not be so cheap that your staff and ministry suffer because you won't give.

16. Today's now day prophets hang up with money.

Successful prophets are not hung up on money. The issue of not understanding money is a prophetic curse. How do you ever expect to be successful? Your gift attracts wealth and prosperity. Prophets who have deep seeded issues with the wealthy, how will you learn from them? You can't learn from what you close yourself off to. You are carrying a staff now, and you did not close yourself off from that, so get pass your hang-up with money so you can learn of it.

You will always learn about money from someone who has more than you. As a prophet, as long as you are constantly adding value to other lives, you will never have any hang-ups about the money you make while doing it *(1 Samuel 9:7; 1 Corinthians 9:7).*

Here are the REAL facts about money:
 A) Money is a vehicle to freedom.
 B) Money is not evil. It doesn't love or hate you, and it's not something magical that "others" have and that you'll never get.
 C) The amount of money you accumulate is in direct correlation to the amount of value you add to the lives of others.

17. Prophets do take calculated risks.

Successful Prophets understand that being a prophet is a calculated risk as life itself. We live it every day as servants of God. We are called to function in a world of sin and not play it on the so-called safe side. Prophet, you must listen to God and know every major decision is never going to bring you major success unless it is in God's plan for your life.

Do the research, take informed risks, and learn when to risk a little in order to win big. That's what we call in the Kingdom of God, faith. Every relevant prophet of God does this! You are relevant. God has you carrying a staff, and you need to govern yourself to the fact that there is work for you to do.

18. Know your resources.

Your staff is a resource; learn how to use it. You will become successful. Prophet realized that God supplies His prophets tools that are designed to get them in the best position to be effective. Successful prophets don't let pride or laziness keep them from making use of their resources. They realize that many times the resource will not look in the traditional way one may expect. Again prophets, if you need help, ask others who have influence where you are at. Mentorship is a blessing!

19. Success is adding value to someone else's life.

Your tenure as a prophet carrying a staff is to add value to someone's life. The very essence of being a successful prophet is to always offers a valuable product for someone's soul. Prophets your work is an exchange of value. Consider all you have been through, and now you carry a staff, a piece of wood that is a tool of God for you to use, which is valuable. Successful prophets understand that they have value *(1 Samuel 9:7)* and that value always adds more value than it costs. This type of mentality will ensure a prophet's success.

20. This is worth doing things because they're hard— avoid 'easy.'

Successful prophets do the hard things. Your staff will provide you with hard challenges, especially early in your life, as you carry it. Learn not to waste anything. Reserve time for the most challenging things in their life.

When something becomes too easy for you, that's a sign you've mastered it and you need to move on to the next task. Take heed as you learn more and more about your staff. Successful prophets know when it is time to move over and start on your next challenge.

21. You live for service to others,

Successful prophets know that if you live solely for yourself, you'll never be satisfied, happy, and successful. But they live and develop for service to better the lives of others; all of their selfish desires will be satisfied beyond their wildest dreams. A life of servitude is, in actuality, a dash of mastery.

Prophet, it doesn't matter who you are; there will be critics. It's human nature, so don't take criticism too hard. Listen, there are hate websites devoted to men and women of God of relevance. Everyone gets criticized, but you can't let that stop you from taking action and moving in faith.

The truth is that people are already talking behind your back, and yes, by taking action, you'll get more people criticizing. Know that it was not your staff. Simply being a prophet yields you this return. Learn how to deal with it. You just have to get over it and realize that once you get past that, you start taking action. This is mental, and to understand this is precious.

The more God exposes you as His servant, the more tools He gives you to work with, the more you will face criticism. Always remember, prophet, what really matters – adding value, not hiding from criticism. When you open up to being vulnerable, you will make huge differences in people's lives. Prophet, do you want to be successful? You carry a staff and become a student of it today.

Let's now discuss the meat of what you will be able to do with your staff. I have outlined that this is personal, and not all of us will operate the same way. In my first book on this topic, I outlined the basic positions of the Prophetic Staff. Now I want to challenge you on the concept of transformation. This is the will of God working through you.

I trust by now you have read the previous six chapters. There is no shame in re-reading them again because now as we move into another phase of mentality and the *Prophetic Staff,* we must now proceed with a level of maturity that is needed to be effective. This is why I will now discuss *The Will of Transformation.*

CHAPTER 7

THE WILL OF TRANSFORMATION

Prophet, there are personal issues that you must understand as you carry a prophetic staff. First, understand that it is the capacity to have a free choice. You can have a choice to be with God or be away from God; that is your choice. No one but you will ultimately control that.

There is your will, and then there is the will of God. The will of a prophet, when it is surrendered to God's will, is always the strongest will. *James 4:1-10* supplies a contrast between a prophet's will submitted and not submitted to God. The bottom line is as we humble ourselves to God, we become candidates for transformation.

Sociologists will speak on the work of the mind, but the mind is a part of the soul of a living being. As prophets, we have a will, and our will has thoughts and feelings. Let's look again at Moses and others who carried a staff and started to pick their minds when they submitted to God; they experienced a personal transformation.

Let's define the will of transformation as the will of God Himself as our minds, will, and emotions, known as our soul, are committed to God for His purposes. As we deal with transformation, many of us were once far from God, and now we are close to Him as we carry His tool of choice for our lives.

Moses is a classic example. The former grandson of Pharaoh, who has been missing for 40 years, is now back and is changed. He is mature, focused, and driven. I never said he was perfect. Some of you will strive for perfection, and I can tell you, you will never make it. God never intended for you to make perfection.

Prophet, study the example of Moses and others who carried staffs and see the evidence of transformation within. This is seen in how a prophet reflects the ways, likeness, and glory of God *(2 Corinthians 3:18)*.

As the now generation prophet, we are sent to people who need deliverance. The foundation of our mentality must be in a good place. When you are in a good place mentally, you will benefit from it as you will start to feel as one with your prophetic staff. This will help you understand that your staff is a part of you, and as you trust God, His power is released upon your situation. God teaches Moses this through His staff as He will teach you also.

Let's face facts today; we have so many things coming at us as we embark with our staff upon the world. I would ask you if you have had an encounter with God that will transform you?

Imagine a simple piece of wood in different forms. Moses' had an encounter with God; he saw a snake. HE is scared, and now he sees an all-powerful God change the snake into a staff. We clearly see Moses knowing that God was and is the all in all. This is a deposited experience for him; the question I ask you is, do you have a deposited experience with God so that you will know that God is able to work through your staff?

Allow me to expand my question. Are you at a level of maturity that will allow you to walk with a staff, pray and minister to people with it? Are you prepared to embark on a level of maturity that may very well will be unmatched by others around you? Have you checked your circles and dealt with the personal issues of your life? No, you will not be perfect, but you have to be mature.

You are about to use a piece of wood that will be transformed into a tool of God at His bidding. You may refer to it as the rod of God, but the reality is it is a piece of wood. The staff is a piece of wood, but when God uses it as His tool, He brings transformation through it.

Just as Moses and Aaron, each one of them carried a "staff or rod" of God. You probably have brothers and sisters who, in the prophetic who have staffs. Should you not, and God has called you, then seek some prophetic fellowship with prophets who know and understand the ministry of the staff. Yes, prophet Moses, held his staff to perform miracles, and his brother Aaron did not hold his staff, and it performed miracles without him also. This is clearly not a joke or anything to be taken lightly.

We want those type of miracles and works today, but we need the mentality to experience miracles. How many of us are really operating in a level of faith that justifies the miracles we seek from God? What I am saying is that we must evaluate ourselves before God constantly, as Moses did. We need this transformation upon us all today.

The reality of a piece of wood that shepherds used and others such as nomads to support the fatigue of the constant journey. Today we see a lot of staffs in the form of walking sticks or maybe fancy canes. I remember being in North Dakota, and a brother there gifted me a diamondback walking stick.

I had no idea how sought-after this type of walking stick was. I was flying home after the revival, and no less than six men stopped me and asked me if I wanted to sell the stick. I am glad I never sold it and still have it. I could not see the reality of what it represented at that time.

Just as the terms rod or staff have been used metaphorically as they allude to the power of God, so I understood the culture of the day, and the diamondback walking stick was the equivalent for the culture I was ministering in.

The presence of God is available for any culture, but I still must stress that the ability to be used by God depends on the servant and the mentality they are operating in. In my first book on this topic, you will see many scriptural references that I will allude to in order to show the reader that the staff is a vital part of prophetic ministry.

There is a passion for the staff throughout scripture. What will make it real and happen in your life will be like David's zeal. He said, "Thy rod and thy staff," as he wrote in the 23rd Psalm. Some felt the rod was for correction, while the staff was a tool for direction.

This denotes God's divine truth and good, which is the assurance that we must embrace as Moses did, or we will not be effective in the use of our staff. This is why we must study the life of Moses and others who embraced the will of transformation.

While I know I am talking about a piece of wood, I am also talking about the prophet who will carry this wood. The prophet and the staff are to operate as one together for what God has called them to do.

The concept of the will of transformation is the standard of your divine calling. It was for Moses, and it will be for you, also. This means you will be empowered to carry out tasks with your staff as Moses and others did.

This is why I have been telling you how personal this is, as it is a direct communication from God to you as it was to Moses that guides you to wield your staff as a tool of God to perform miracles.

As I did in my first book on this topic, your rod or staff is still a piece of wood. That wood that is used as a staff is a dead piece of wood, as you already know, but it is alive with the presence of God upon it as God sees fit. That same staff is now a symbolic tool of God that functions on the prophet's faith and obedience of the prophet, and that is you. You're looking for the supernatural, and you have it upon your life.

This means that you can now manipulate the elements around you, which is an awesome sight to see. Let me be clear. You will not just arrive at this point but earn your way to this level. This is why the focus is on the prophet to mature.

This is not a novice prophetic showpiece. The danger of not understanding the will of transformation is that a prophet will spend time working on a staff, preparing it, and then after it is presented to God, you take the staff home and put it in a corner to collect dust.

This is so totally not acceptable. This proves that you do not know or appreciate what you may have at your hands. Most of all, it is an insult to God as you claimed God said this and God said that, and you are not concerned at all about your learning and understanding the ministry of the *Prophetic Staff.*

We must understand that we go as far as our prophetic development is concerned. This is a simply awesome opportunity that God has given us. God has no respect for person, so as we look at and study Moses, we see the authority he operated in and as we claim our calling of the prophetic staff.

We must be reminded that the will of transformation can grant the prophet the opportunity to elevate over any situation they face. Prophet stop reading for a moment and start to ponder and understand the concept of the supernatural that is represented in the staff that you carry, the staff Moses carried, the staff of Aaron, and the staff of others.

Can you see God patiently working with each of us if we mean business? God will give us experiences and supernatural guidance, and He will be the guiding force that we will need to operate efficiently for His purposes.

The will of transformation is the action of the anointing upon God's prophet in the same way we saw it upon Moses. Did you notice that Aarons' staff did not work exactly like that of Moses? This is critical as we have now seen how personal this walk with God is. This is very personal, yet God allows us to find and have fellowship with other prophets and seers who are assigned to walk with staffs. Prophet, allow me to share with you some practical prophetic exercises needed to help develop your prophetic staff ministry.

Chapter 8 is on prophetic exercises and will not benefit you unless you are mentally ready to do them. Prophet, are you really ready to grow and awaken in the anointing of God in a new season of your life?

PROPHETIC STAFF EXERCISES

The will of transformation is real, and it works, but like I have said over and over in this book, there has to be a foundation within the prophet. Let's recap; we have discussed various steps and angles of mentality that are needed and necessary.

Yes, you may be alone. Yes, you may be the odd one, but that is who God has called you to be. So if you are seen a certain way, the only way that matters is how God sees you and your zeal to accomplish the assignment that God has given you. My focus is still on your mentality because if you have not been beaten mentally, you are a candidate for such a life reality.

Allow me to present some prophetic exercises that are needed for any prophet who has been assigned by God to walk with a prophetic staff. None of us are exempt, and the key is for you and your staff to become as one for the purposes of God.

Prayer And Meditation

While this should be a daily routine, ensure that you set aside time with your staff for prayer and meditation. You should practice the various positions that are outlined in *The Prophetic Staff.*

You are seeking an even deeper connection with God as you see to have your spiritual eyes open and your ears in tune with God's insight. While I know some of you feel you do this daily, I would encourage you to set aside some special time for your prophetic staff; you must get used to it.

Practice Listening To God

Commit to sitting in silence for short periods of time to simply listen to God. Enjoy the solitude. Speak to God and seek His answers. Ask God about your staff. Become attentive to the thoughts and impressions of the moments in His presence. This will surely help you align with God's word, and it will enrich your character.

Study Scripture Daily

Here you need to really focus on the lives of the biblical prophets. Read scriptures that you know and ones you do not know. Pay attention to the slightest of details. Spend time as you meditate on scriptures, especially ones on prophecy. Read and re-read *1 Thessalonians 5* and *1st Corinthians 14* as you come to understand more about the actual purpose of the prophecy.

Prophetic Journaling

Prophet, as you seek God, write down not just your dreams, but write down your thoughts, impressions, and ideas daily. This is important as you see yourself growing daily as your communication with God grows more and more. This can be done on a notepad or an electronic device, but it is necessary in order for you to see patterns within your life. Prophet, you must journal; this is critical.

Seek Prophetic Confirmation

This is where your relationships are so important. Seek your leadership to share what you are thinking and seeing over selected periods of time. This must be a trusted relationship, and some things that are spoken should not be shared anywhere else.

The purpose here is to get feedback and insight into what you are receiving daily. Prophet, this will make or break you. This is your choice, but prophets who do this experience different patterns of growth into their mantle.

Prophetic Activation Work

Your ability to work with others within a group of like-minded prophets is important and critical. As we look and study the school of the prophets in scripture, we see this fact in situations like "death in the pot and the axe head floats." All involved prophets and all were on the same sheet of much despite the issues of their human imperfections.

This type of interaction will be a blessing to you and enhance your personal self-value assessment of yourself. You will have the insight to add to your personal circle of prophets you interact with. This will help you find yourself as you will be in the atmosphere of others with the same concerns.

Prophetic Meetings

Prophetic meetings are invaluable if you understand why they happen. This is an opportunity to come and be empowered within the company of your peers and leaders who are seasoned and understand exactly what you are going through.

The meetings help fill the void of being alone. Although, they are positioned to elevate the prophet and allow mistakes within an environment geared to personal one-on-one development in group seating.

The impartations, declarations, and genuine fellowship are needed and worth the investment you may make, especially if you carry a staff and the leaders of the school employ staffs also.

What is so important that you understand is the fact that you are now becoming the best version of yourself. You, with all your issues and problems, are on your way. This, I say again, is personal, and yet you have the gift that God has put into your life for you to function.

Walking with a prophetic staff is not easy; it is a hard prophetic assignment for this day and time. Mentally you must be ready. Please note that throughout this book, I have pounded you on the fact of being ready mentally. The prophet who is ready mentally is also spiritually sound and ready to be the exponent of God for His purposes.

Any gift in the prophetic is a work in progress. Those of you who will carry a staff must understand you must have patience with yourself. I have communicated to you in earlier chapters that while we all carry staffs, we may have various different individual assignments.

Some of us may carry our staffs more than others. Some of us may use our staffs more than others. The key is to find your good place within you as you carry a prophetic staff. This piece of wood is for more than show. It really is a tool of God.

I have mainly discussed various exercises that every prophet and non-prophetic staff carriers, should practice to elevate their gifts. Let me now give some wisdom that is essential to your growth.

No one should hold or play with your staff unless you are led by God to allow them. Let me say that again, no one. The only exceptions should be your leadership, who carry staffs themselves. The warfare is too great to allow your staff to be a toy for kids or a conversation piece for unknowing observers. I cannot stress how important this is.

The only other authorized person to handle your staff should be a peer or an assistant who has known and walked with you for several years. Seven to 10 years is the starting point. Do not allow anyone except the already mentioned to handle or play with your staff.

Keep your staff protected. Invest in a cloth cover and a hard cover to go over that. This will be excellent when you travel, especially needed when you fly. Prophet, be prepared to pay the extra fee for the staff; you will need to pay it unless you have your own private jet.

As you invest in a hardcover for your staff, normally, sporting goods stores are the perfect location for that. The fishing rod covers are usually durable enough to provide adequate protection for your staff. Make sure you do this.

You should inquire with your senior leadership for insight if you need to ensure you have the adequate protection of your staff. Once you know that you have adequate covering, you can allow an assistant to carry your staff in this manner, but only allow them to touch your staff if they have walked with you for 7-10 years at least. The only exception will and should be your senior leadership. You need to be clear on this before you proceed.

Please refer to The Prophetic Staff, the first book I wrote on this subject for the construction of your staff. You should be able to help others construct their staffs after you read *The Prophetic Staff.* Be advised interested prophets will ask and inquire with you. Be prepared to talk with them about your prophetic staff.

Treat your staff like you treat your Bible; it is precious. Your staff is precious. Your staff is a vital part of your ministry. You may need to use it at any time. Again take your time and find yourself with your staff; it will be worth it.

Prophet, you should read and know this information, so please take it to heart and allow yourself to grow. This is so about your personal individual growth and what God is doing in your life.

Sooner or later, you will be faced with your peers who do not carry a staff. How do you relate to them? How do you share with them? Let me now offer you some vital points in your dealing with your peers who do not carry a staff. This is what mends us together as prophets and allows us to bond and empower each other.

CHAPTER 9

MY STAFF VERSUS MY NON STAFF PEERS

Let us never forget we are in the relationship-building business. Relationships are a vital part of our ministries, especially within our peer groups and the prophetic community. One of the issues that has crippled the prophetic community as a whole is our non-existent communication among groups.

The sad fact is that a significant number of now generations of prophets tend to play games and can be very judgmental of each other. Why? Because we have different types of gifts and have not learned how to respect other gifts. Many times it takes a minor miracle for us to have the fellowship we do have. We are like mother hens protecting our small hens.

The reality is yes, there are many reasons for this, and yes, I can see it, and I am aware of many of the situations. I like many of you, do understand many of the reasons why. The reality is that we are still works in progress. Would you agree with me that despite our situations, we must push to move forth?

I say all this because when you look at our now day prophetic community, we have multiple great divides in our teaching, beliefs, and cultures. Let me encourage you to read my book *"Prophet Sent to a Cross Culture"* to understand this better.

Now, how about the prophets who carry a staff versus those who do not? How do we approach them, how do we relate to them, and could we consider how we may be able to close the gaps within our prophetic community?

Those of you who are emerging prophets may not be fully aware of these complex issues, but you see things within your emerging circles. We have been given such a wonderful spectrum to work for God in, and we also bear the burden of making it better as we get better as individuals and as groups of godly influence. We are responsible for the culture of the prophetic community.

As I start, we now must figure out how to deal with our peers who do not have prophetic staffs. We must be able to relate to them. So let's set ourselves in agreement and let's talk about ways that we can relate to prophets who may not be educated nor understand why the purpose of carrying staffs is relevant. Keep in mind this is not to recruit, but it is to empower.

We allow God to pick and choose whom He calls for His purposes. Let's start by introducing your peers to your staff in an atmosphere that is conducive to learning and growing. Look for this to be probably in a prophetic school or a prophetic conference. This can even be an informal meeting or gathering as long as the theme of growth is at the forefront. We must be guarded on the atmosphere and the place to share on the staff.

This is why we must respect our initial communication because it is the first impression we may make and may be a lasting impression on our peers. Our knowledge should reflect direct references from scripture. Whether they are senior, mature, or emerging prophets, they know that our base issues as to why we walk with a staff can be reflected in scripture. They can see how God has arranged and empowered us for His purposes.

Keep this in mind. There are enough issues in the prophetic that are unscriptural, so we need to reflect scripture to our peers who do not carry or understand staffs. The biggest reason we share is to reflect that the staff is a tool of God and not a fad. This piece of wood is to be respected highly.

Those of you who are experienced can share on the fact of how your staff enhances your ministry. Please share this. Prophets who do not use a prophetic staff will appreciate the fact of how your staff enhances your ministry, and this will give them insight on any tool that God will give them to use in their ministries.

This is why it will be personal, and that is needed. We all are different, but your personal story may help me or any other prophet, especially a prophet who does not carry a prophetic staff. This book has been written to help elevate the ministry and platform of the prophetic staff. There are prophets and those in general who want to know more about the prophetic staff.

This is why prophets who have staffs and prophets who do not have staffs can help each other. I can't stress how vital your personal story is, and that is why a deposited experience is needed so you can help educate and elevate your peer prophets. There is no doubt that this type of exchange fosters a deeper understanding between prophets and bridges respect. The prophetic needs this. There is no doubt.

This can and will enhance the personal differences between prophets and let your peers know that it is a choice why you carry the prophetic staff. This is a choice that you made to obey God, which teaches that God speaks to all His prophets.

The reality is that He does not give every prophet the same mantle or the same assignment. Can you see how much stronger our prophetic community would be if we could be successful in getting this message across?

We have the opportunity to be trail blazers if we will only execute and do it in love. Respect and love are clearly lacking in our prophetic communities, and we need to be able to pass that along. Can you imagine showing an emerging prophet various positions of how the staff was used and what God has done with your staff as you have used it to minister to His people? This is your opportunity to let the God in you shine for His sake.

Now we are boarding the horizons of all concerned. The prophets who do not carry a staff are now being shown respect and love because you are open to showing them what God is doing in your life. They now can be open to you and ask questions, and learning can continue. We do not have enough of this in the prophetic, and you can, with your staff, be God's spokesperson. This is simply awesome.

We are in a business of nonstop learning, and the sooner we realize that, the better off we will be. None of us are immune to learning, which is true for the most seasoned senior prophet you or I may know.

I am well aware that you may encounter non-prophetic staff prophets who will reject your teaching and may even insult your work. Listen, prophet, we are dealing with human beings, and if we are caring for a prophetic staff, our skin should not be so thin or sensitive either. Do understand the way you may be received may also reflect on the type of prophet before you.

I want to challenge you to look at the now day prophets as a whole. Let's look at the prophets who have credit issues; we will see so many of them have problems giving and problems with teachings on prosperity spurred by God's prophetic gift.

There is a connection here and whether we want to deal with it or not, it reflects on us as seers and prophets. Our personal habits are displayed in your ministries. This is why you and I must become the best versions of ourselves. We must dig deep and strive to be at our best at all times, despite what is happening in our lives.

On a final point, we can feel a freeness to demonstrate what God is doing. We can do this outside of resistance or general ignorance because we did not communicate when given the opportunity. When we share, think about the fact that because you shared, there are prophetic peers who are now praying for your success as you use your staff.

Generationally it seems we have lost this type of edge in the prophetic community. God wants us now to regain it. The latter part of *Hosea 4:6* explains that we cannot give to our kids what we don't have. Generational ignorance is not an option. Your prophetic staff gives you an opportunity to educate and facilitate unseen and unrealized ways that God is moving today in our lives.

Prophets, we must prepare ourselves, as this will take time and effort. Each one of us needs to know and realize this. We need to be at our best in order to help others. The standard, if it is anything less, is not acceptable.

Allow me to share this. The ability to help others for a prophet assigned to carry a staff rest on these seven essential points. Read and absorb them.

1. Master the prophetic skill you have: Seek to learn more. You must dedicate time and study to your staff and ministry. You must keep yourself sharp. The responsibility rests upon you. You will have to make the sacrifice.

Have you noticed how we make sacrifices for the world and the pursuit of happiness? The energy we produce for the world has to be put into our efforts for the mastery of what God has given us.

2. Prophet, your ethical conduct must always be at a high standard: You are always being watched. Your ability to express and exercise your confidentiality is priceless. This includes the way you carry yourself.

3. Empathy for others: This is a quality that is needed. Genuine care and concern are revealed in how you listen and communicate with others is a strong quality that must be developed. Remember, this is a personal issue of development with you and every prophet you know.

4. Prophetic Self-Expression: You realize that you are unique and different from all others. We now see you as the best version of yourself because of your confidence. Be authentic and embrace the fact that you are.

5. Prophetic Community Engagement: Use your platform to elevate whatever God gives you. Seek revelation and know that it can come in different ways. Overlook nothing. What God gives you may elevate the entire prophetic community. This is why you study, so you can grow and share. Never be afraid to do that.

6. Learn how to Adapt: The world is changing constantly. This type of change is coming hard, and it is almost daily. We are in this world, but we are not of this world. We have adapted to cell phones, Wi-Fi, laptops, 24 hours a day camera, and many other things.

I forgot to mention Tik Tok, Instagram, Facebook, Twitter, and numerous other platforms. We are still able to share our message for God. We must learn and continue to do what we are called to do.

7. Constantly Review: Points 1-6 need to be done over and over as your growth is your responsibility. You can carry a staff for show, or you can carry your staff for God. Your ability to test yourself and demonstrate points 1-6 speaks volumes about how you relate to God and others.

Now that we have reviewed these points. Let us now look to the future. You are a prophet carrying a staff. Now let's look at your national or international assignment and prepare you for the challenges ahead.

CHAPTER 10

THE STAFF, THE PROPHET, THE CHALLENGE

What happens in your life when you're in a position that has been designated for you? Think of it as your status that has identified you as a prophet called to the nations. You have a prophetic staff, and in your eyes, things are falling into place.

While everything seems to be in place, but the reality is that you're in a place that contradicts what your status says and where you're supposed to be going; you are stuck, but you're a prophet to the nations.

Here is what will be your greatest challenge moving forth. Your reality is a small place where people know you and may not even like you. This is the type of world that God has chosen to bring up His prophets in. This includes you and I also. The prophet who has been called to the nations in a place that looks like anything but that.

The reality of being in a place or a situation where your prophetic ministry looks different than others around you. You have a staff, and others do not. People are testing you daily. Norms, customs, and the traditions of where you are can and will wear on you.

You are called to the nations but the platform you're on is redundant and in the back of your mind, you really do question even if you're really called to the nations. How do you deal with this, knowing that you are being called to a larger platform than you see yourself on, but you have no reference point?

What will help the prophet in this situation is to learn and understand that the mundane times we live in between the mountain top or the outright glory experiences of God are equally important. The key is to understand and execute in the moment as God would have you grow. This is why your prophetic staff will teach you that things are not always as they look. Prophet, the lessons of your staff will identify you quicker than you think.

1 Samuel 17:17 sets the stage for understanding how to function in a small place or situation when God has called you to a larger status. You find yourself going through storms that you must be skillful in while navigating through the storms.

David has been called by his stepfather, Jessie, to take food to his brothers: bread, cheese, and corn. David is a delivery boy for his brothers. He has been called to serve them. David goes to the trench where the battle was between the Philistines and the Israelites.

David sees the champion of the Philistines, and he sees the fear of his countrymen also. He also encounters conversations between his fellow countrymen. David is in the middle of listening to opinions and perspectives that he does not necessarily agree with. Look at David. He wants to know what is going to be done.

David hears and expresses his concerns, and even his brother approaches him and challenges him and his presence in a place that is supposed to be reserved for warriors. David questions his brother, and he sets the stage for us as we look at a prophetic figure that no one seems to know how to handle. This sounds like us with our prophetic staffs and no one knows how to communicate with us because they think we are weird or super crazy.

Does this sound like you? You're in the middle of people who know you. They know about you, and nothing they do or say will encourage you to achieve the assignment you have upon your life.

For many of us who were at a meeting, and it was announced by a prophet or seer who came into your area. For David, his calling had been identified by Samuel as he visited his home for the next king of Israel to be identified. Samuel identifies him in 1 Samuel 16 as the next king of Israel. At this time, his brothers are not very fond of him, especially his older brother who questions his presence in what was supposed to be a war zone.

A status has been given to David. No one, not even his family, understands the next steps for the life of David. You must see here that David is looked upon as insignificant. Imagine a future king doing such small assignments on a small scale. Serving lunch, oh no.

The new generation would have a problem with such a task today, as the assignment most clearly does not match the new status of David, nor would it match a now day prophet called to the nations.

The reality is we can't see the significance of small tasks. The small tasks are just as important as the large ones everyone sees and swoons over. Learning your staff will teach and instruct you on the small things; that is a fact. These things will be vital to your understanding your challenge ahead in your calling as a prophet called to the nations.

This means you, like us all, have a challenge ahead and are obligated to meet the challenge. Let me challenge you in this chapter as a Prophet Called to the Nations with a Prophetic Staff; how do you handle it? Now is the time to assume you have your life together, as this chapter is unlike the others because now you have people looking at you and following you.

The challenge ahead of you is not going anywhere.

1. Effective and Relevant Prophets, with National / International Callings upon their lives, do little things with excellence. They understand the importance of normal things. They are standard bearers. This includes their staffs and any other special gift from God.

They practice excellence in the mundane days and times of life. God gives you practice with little responsibility. This is so hard to understand.

Stop complaining and griping about the little things in life. The little things get you ready for the big things in life. Your light afflictions prepare you with confidence and courage. How do you define greatness? You must know that God is with you, and He is clearly bigger than you can reason. Despise not the day of small beginnings. The little things determine what is coming next in your life.

Prophet, you're not ready to go to the nations until you understand the timing that everything in your life is important, no matter how little or how big. You must master the details of destiny and time.

2. As a prophet to the nations, showing up in half the battle. Your ability to show up and be accountable is priceless. You may not have all the solutions or all the answers. But the ability to show up and be accountable is something the enemy of the prophet does not want the prophet to realize.

David showing up as he needed provided the timely preparation of God in his life for future realities. Remember, he could have been big-headed and not shown up because he was anointed to be the next king as this time. Many of us find it hard to realize that what we do matters, including the small issues. Can you imagine God is planning your life and has been planning your life for times before you were even born?

God starts you out as a kid or as an ordinary person. You're a kid. You're normal, and maybe no one knows you or knows of you, and now you find yourself and your life-changing in a moment, which leads to another moment. Welcome to the Ministry of the Prophetic Staff. This is precisely what I am describing. Moses and others dealt with it, and so shall you also.

This is the process of God as He orchestrated our lives as prophets, seers, watchmen, and apostles. The moments of life are what connect us to our greatness. Therefore, so many prophets called to the nations never go. They don't go because they miss the moment. How do they miss it?

When they say I don't want to do this, or I don't want to do that. When they feel they don't need to give this or that. When they feel certain issues or tasks are beneath them. Some of you are coming into a moment of destiny. Sometimes the small things stop you from developing in other areas.

3. The prophet that has providence. Providence makes sense out of the nonsense of life. The ability to not overlook things is important to the prophet of God. God has a purpose and plan, and what seems to not be important to your issues are critical to your development. The spirit of ignore has cost more prophets their lives and destinies. Your staff training will allow you to not overlook things.

How many of us understand that having providence in our lives show the strategies of God? The who, what, and the where and even when nothing makes sense, is still God doing what He does. What you do, your grandchildren or great-grand may or may not benefit from your life. God is always in control.

David goes to the battlefield with lunch, and it was his legacy. The right place and the right time in your life equals your destiny. Let me encourage you. Your walking with a staff is the tool of miracles, signs, and wonders in your life.

The right place and the right time is where David met and saw Goliath for the first time. David hears Goliath speak and insult the people of Israel and is affected by his words. This is the equivalent of having a great anointing and what seems like no place to use it.

You may think of yourself as having a huge vision and no resources. Why would God give me this vision, prophetic staff, and gift, but there is nowhere to use it? Your calling is great, but your ministry is small; your insight is uncanny, but no one listens to you. Can you see your challenge here?

Take this to another level, and while no one is listening to you, God positions you to serve people who do not even like you. Who liked David among his brothers? Who showed him love? Remember David, according to Psalm 69: 5; it is David who confesses the sins of his mom. He speaks about the affair of his mom. David is a prophet, just like you, with issues around his life that present constant challenges.

This is a classic example of how God is taking the prophets through the process. You are learning with your staff, and there are multiple challenges ahead. Developing a prophet is to stretch, to identify who will and who will not. Can you understand God's process?

The key is to allow God to process you. God knows clearly where you're at and why He has you there. You want God to move you to the nations; you must understand the necessary training that must be done in and through your life.

Can you imagine God speaking to those prophets who are feeling inadequate in small places or situations, and He is using them as he used David? They have been given big visions and no one to support them.

Your staff has afforded you plenty of haters or many who misunderstand. He puts you in a church, and everyone turns on you. He exposes your calling to your family, who ridicule and reject you. You do understand that many may have not been exposed to staff ministry. Can you see the challenge again?

You are not crazy. You're called. The issue is that God is looking for you to look to Him and not the world. People will come against you and criticize you but understand that what they do does not matter because it will not change the plans nor the decision of God for your life.

The place, situation, how you feel about someone, and your perspective on another prophet's gift does not matter. This is the prophet's mentality on the prophetic staff. The only thing that matters is that you're in a place or a situation that God has you in. He controls your destiny, and His placement is for His purposes.

We can ask David for his perspective, and he will tell you he went through a process to become as God had chosen him to be a king among all his other gifts, especially his prophetic gift. God took him through a unique process on his way to destiny.

Look at yourself; you're a prophet called to the nations, and you're in a small situation and a small place where you're misunderstood, not appreciated, and flat-out despised. You come to the truth that God has you where He wants you, and as He told Paul, my grace is sufficient. You are the prophet, with the staff and the challenge.

ABOUT THE AUTHOR

Apostle Ken Cox started serving God in 1994 after a series of unforeseen life failures. Out of the military and seemly starting life over again, by 2000, Apostle Cox had found his life calling as a Prophet. The challenge of learning and understanding presented a new frontier. Apostle Cox dove into the process and has now emerged as a well-traveled prophet who serves the Body of Christ as an Apostle.

Apostle Cox, along with his wife, Prophetess Sabina Cox are the leaders of Where Eagles Fly Fellowship Inc., a fellowship of prophets and apostle across the USA and beyond who are dedicated and focused on establishing the prophetic gift back into society as they raise up prophets around the country and abroad.

Apostle Cox and Prophetess Cox are available for Revivals, Conferences and Meetings. They have been featured in meetings and sought-after to teach and instruct the prophetic for ministries seeking to learn more about the gift. Apostle and Prophetess Cox have 3 children and 4 grandkids as of this writing and currently reside in Durham, NC. Contact them through the Where Eagles Fly office at 919-695-3375 or 919-213-1328 or at www.whereeaglesfly.us.

www.ingramcontent.com/pod-product-compliance
Lightning Source LLC
Chambersburg PA
CBHW071024120626
46546CB00003B/1211